NUTSHELLS

ENGLISH LEGAL SYSTEM IN A NUTSHELL

AUSTRALIA
LBC Information Services
Sydney

CANADA
Carswell
Toronto • Ontario

NEW ZEALAND
Brookers
Auckland

SINGAPORE AND MALAYSIA
Thomson Information (S.E.) Asia
Singapore

NUTSHELLS

ENGLISH LEGAL SYSTEM IN A NUTSHELL

FIFTH EDITION

by

PENNY DARBYSHIRE
Ph.D., M.A.
Senior Lecturer in Law, Kingston Law School,
Kingston University

London • Sweet & Maxwell • 2001

Published in 2001 by
Sweet & Maxwell Limited of
100 Avenue Road, Swiss Cottage, London, NW3 3PF
(http://www.sweetandmaxwell.co.uk)
Computerset by
Wyvern 21 Ltd, Bristol
Printed in Italy by Legoprint S.p.A. Lavis, Trento

A CIP Catalogue record
for this book is available
from the British Library

ISBN 0–421–74280–1

CONTENTS

1. INSTITUTIONS

THE COURT STRUCTURE

The most striking points about the English court structure are that:

1. It is not a faultlessly coherent and single, logically developed "system." It grew piecemeal and various parts of it have been reformed and reshaped to suit the perceived needs of the time. The existing structure is so taken for granted, however, that until very recently it seemed almost heretical to question whether we need two levels of criminal courts of first instance and three civil first instance courts, with jurisdictions overlapping.

2. Most civil cases are not heard in the civil courts at all but in one of the major alternative forums which have proliferated in the twentieth century, *i.e.* tribunals and arbitration. The distribution of work between courts and tribunals is a little arbitrary but has not been questioned since the Franks Committee Report in 1957.

It has been left to academics to raise the question of whether the popularity of alternatives is not a reflection on the shortcomings of the civil courts and procedure. Recently, however, civil procedure has been radically reformed by the Civil Procedure Rules 1998, following the recommendations of Lord Woolf in *Access to Justice*, 1996, better known as "The Woolf Report". Criminal procedure is under similar radical scrutiny in 2000 by Auld L.J. Look out for his report in 2001.

Criminal Courts

Magistrates' courts. These can be seen as the most important courts as far as the public are concerned because, to most people, being involved in a court case means being dealt with by magistrates. There, almost all criminal cases commence and about 97 per cent are disposed of. Magistrates impose 95 per cent of all sentences.

In Outer London and the provinces, most cases are heard by lay justices, sitting in twos or threes, advised by a justices' clerk or court clerk. In Inner London, most cases are heard by a district judge (magistrates' courts), advised by a clerk. Most London clerks are professionally qualified. There are over 300 lay justices in Inner London.

Magistrates and their clerks wear ordinary clothes and no wigs and so do the barristers and solicitors appearing before them. Of their criminal case load, about half are road traffic offences, most of which are decided in the absence of the defendant, who may plead guilty by post. Another quarter are "offences triable either way," *i.e.* cases of median seriousness, where the defendant has the option of a Crown Court appearance instead. The rest are other summary offences. Magistrates hear almost all juvenile criminal cases. These are dealt with in private by specialist magistrates in the youth court.

There are over 30,300 magistrates, who sit part-time in around 350 Benches in England and Wales. Many of the very small, rural Benches have been analgamated in the 1990s. Cities such as Manchester and Birmingham may have over 20 courtrooms in use simultaneously. Magistrates' maximum sentencing powers are six months' imprisonment and a £5,000 fine from the adult court and two years' detention from the youth court.

Criticisms. 1. It is an accident of history that most cases are dealt with in Inner London by a professional magistrate, advised by a professionally qualified clerk, yet in Outer London and the provinces the same work is done by lay justices who are advised mostly by court clerks, many of whom are not barristers or solicitors.

2. As the lay justices depend on their clerk for legal and practical advice, he may be tempted to interfere in factual or sentencing decisions.

3. Disparity exists in sentencing between magistrates' courts. Magistrates would defend themselves by saying that these are local courts serving local needs so sentencing will vary from town to town.

4. Since criminal cases have been redistributed from the Crown Court, in the Criminal Law Act 1977 and later legislation, magistrates deal with the bulk of criminal cases, including some very serious ones but criminal law and evidence continue to develop as if criminal cases were mostly decided by judge and jury.

The Crown Court. The Crown Court is the criminal court of first instance which deals with the most serious (indictable) offences, as well as some of those triable either way. These together comprise around two to three per cent of all criminal cases. It also has an appellate jurisdiction (see Chapter 5). The drama of jury trial in the Crown Court captures the public imagination and its buildings, furniture, judges and barristers' garb all add to the attraction of a serious criminal trial. The Central Criminal Court ("Old Bailey") is the Crown Court centre which attracts most public attention.

The Crown Court was created by the Courts Act 1971. Note there is one *single* Crown Court, which is divided between around 90 centres throughout England and Wales.

The six circuits, which evolved historically, still exist for administrative purposes. The Crown Court is divided into three tiers, as follows:

First tier High Court judges deal with the most serious offences here, as well as civil High Court cases. Circuit judges, recorders and assistant recorders may also sit here.

Second tier High Court judges, circuit judges, and recorders and assistant recorders deal with criminal cases only.

Third tier Circuit judges, recorders and assistant recorders deal with criminal cases.

The consultation paper *Transforming The Crown Court*, 1999, suggests doing away with these tiers.

Criticisms. 1. The importance of jury trial in the Crown Court is exaggerated (see section on the jury, Chapter 3).

2. Why preserve two criminal courts of first instance? (See below).

The Queen's Bench Division of the High Court. This division features in the criminal court structure because its Divisional Court, consisting of three High Court judges, deals with appeals by way of case stated from the magistrates' court and Crown Court and it exercises supervisory jurisdiction over all inferior courts, *i.e.* reviewing the legality of their proceedings and orders. The QBD sits centrally in the Strand and in 24 provincial Crown Court centres. Additionally, non-contested QBD cases are heard at many county court centres.

The Court of Appeal (Criminal Division). This was formed in 1966, replacing the Court of Criminal Appeal. For most purposes, the court is composed of three or more Lords Justices and/or High Court judges. Appeals against sentence may be dealt with by two and other applications by one judge. The court hears appeals of both fact and law (see Chapter 5). Until 1997 it sat only in the Royal Courts of Justice in the Strand but Lord Chief Justice Bingham took the Court of Appeal to hear cases in Liverpool and Bristol (1999). Of course, several Courts of Appeal usually sit simultaneously.

The House of Lords (Appellate Committee). The House of Lords' jurisdiction is not confined to the English legal system, in that it also hears appeals from Scotland and Northern Ireland. The minimum number of judges to determine an appeal is three but is normally five. Apart from the Lords of Appeal in Ordinary (Law Lords), ex-Law Lords, ex-Lord Chancellors, ex-judicial Privy Councillors and other ex-superior judges may sit, although they almost never do. Recently, Lord Chancellors have refrained from sitting but Lord Hailsham sat occasionally and Lord Mackay sat several times as had Lord Irvine. The Law Lords do not specialise but, in practice, appeals from Scotland are heard by at least one Scottish Law Lord and Chancery appeals by at least one Chancery judge.

Appeals are heard in a committee room of the House of Lords and the Law Lords wear lounge suits.

The Privy Council (Judicial Committee). This was formed in 1833. It hears appeals from some Commonwealth countries, including republics. It also hears appeals from the General Medical Council and other professional bodies and gained jurisdiction in devolution matters in 1998. It comprises the Lord President of the Council, the Lord Chancellor, Law Lords, Privy Councillors and former Councillors who have held high judicial office and Privy Councillors who hold or have held high judicial office in the Commonwealth.

Criticism. The Law Lords, who often provide a battery of barely reconcilable opinions in the House of Lords are forced, when sitting as the Privy Council, to produce one opinion, with one permissible dissent. Some raise the question as to why they cannot do this, as they sometimes do, when wearing their House of Lords hats, and make life easier for the rest of us, who have to apply their Lordships' opinions.

This argument is countered by Law Lords like Lord Reid, who thought the single Privy Council judgments inferior, being "no more than the highest common factor of all the views." Further, other opponents cite the example of the European Court of Justice which, it is argued, in having to reach one judgment between its 15 judges, produces a bland amalgam which is difficult of application. Commentators here and abroad suggest the P.C.'s jurisdiction in death penalty appeals from the Caribbean is inappropriate for modern, European judges.

The European Court of Justice. The details of the court's powers are dealt with in Chapters 2 and 5. It consists of 15 judges. For the most important cases they all sit together. One peculiar feature, unknown to English law, is the function of the eight advocates general. These are independent individuals from member states, qualified for high judicial office, or equivalent. One sits with the bench in each hearing and may question the parties, delivering an opinion some weeks later. This sets out facts, law and a suggested judgment. There is a European Court of First Instance whose 15 judges hear staff cases and applications for judicial review and damages.

The ECJ hears:

(a) applications from member states' courts for preliminary rulings under Article 234 EEC (see below);
(b) direct actions against member states or E.C. institutions;
(c) requests for opinions on international law and the EEC Treaties;
(d) tort claims;
(e) actions for judicial review.

The European Court of Human Rights. This court enforces the European Convention on Human Rights, which includes such rights as liberty, security, fair trial, freedom of thought, conscience, assembly, etc., right to life, right not to be subjected to torture or inhuman or degrading treatment, etc. The United Kingdom, being a signatory to the European Convention, has subjected itself to this court's jurisdiction but the Convention did not become part of U.K. law until 2000, when the Human Rights Act 1998 came into force. The United Kingdom has been taken before the court on many occasions, necessitating amendments in domestic law, *e.g.* with regard to prison correspondence, treatment of prisoners in Northern Ireland, contempt, etc. Students regularly confuse this with the European Court of Justice, an

E.U. institution, although the ECHR is quite independent of the E.C.

Civil Courts

The civil court structure includes the House of Lords, ECJ and Privy Council, all of which have been described, in full, above. There is little to say on the CA (Civil Division) which is not said in Chapter 5. The CA (Civil Division) normally sits in the Royal Courts of Justice but also sat in Cardiff in 1999.

The magistrates' court. This has been described above but it must be remembered that magistrates have a very significant civil case load, the predominant part being family cases. Lay justices who conduct family proceedings are selected from specially trained panels within each Bench, as for the youth court. They are empowered to make and enforce most orders ancillary or preliminary to a divorce, *e.g.* separation. Magistrates also have a wide jurisdiction under the Children Act 1989 and can, for example, make adoption and care orders. Their remaining civil jurisdiction includes such items as council tax enforcement. They also have an administrative function, licensing (*e.g.* liquor licensing), which is a remnant of the days when lay justices performed local government functions.

The county courts. These courts were created in 1846, in response to criticisms of the predecessors of the High Court: that civil actions were expensive and inconvenient, being centralised, making justice inaccessible to ordinary civil litigants. The modern county courts (around 260) are thus a cheap, locally-based alternative to the High Court. Their jurisdiction is set out in the C.L.S.A. 1990 and the Civil Procedure Rules 1999 (see below). They are entirely civil and their case load consists of contract, tort, especially personal injuries, property, divorce and other family matters, bankruptcy, admiralty, equity and race relations, etc. Many county court cases are claims for debts. Like the magistrates' courts, the county courts are very significant to the public in terms of their workload.

Small claims in the county court (under £5,000) are dealt with by a special simple and cheap procedure. Solicitors have had rights of audience in the county court since its creation.

Criticisms. See the Civil Justice Review and the Woolf Report (below).

The High Court.

The High Court is situated in the Royal Courts of Justice (Strand) and 24 provincial (Crown Court) centres in the six court circuits.

The Queen's Bench Division. This is the largest, generalist division, consisting of the Lord Chief Justice and 70 puisne judges. It deals with common law, *e.g.* tort, contract, debt and personal injuries. It contains two specialist courts: Admiralty and Commercial.

Divisional Court. This court hears appeals and exercises the supervisory jurisdiction, judicially reviewing the legality of the actions of both inferior courts and the executive. Since the 1980s, administrative law (public law) cases have been listed together in the Crown Office List and dealt with by a group of specialist judges within the QBD. **Note**: there are also Divisional Courts in the other two High Court divisions.)

The Chancery Division. This is the successor to the Chancellor's court, dispensing equity. Here the Vice-Chancellor and 18 puisne judges hear claims relating to property, trusts, wills, partnerships, revenue, contentious probate and bankruptcies. It includes two specialist courts, Patent and Companies and the Division sits in London and in eight provincial centres.

The Family Division. This was created in 1970. It consists of the President and 17 puisne judges, who hear divorce cases and ancillary matters and Children Act cases in London and over 50 provincial centres.

Specialist Jurisdictions

The Restrictive Practices Court is independent of the High Court but consists of High Court judges and lay people. It sits rarely and hears cases relating to restrictive practices and fair trading.

The Technology and Construction Court takes complex technical or factual cases from the QBD or Chancery, mainly building contracts and computer disputes, which are heard by circuit judges.

The Court of Protection manages the property of those lacking in mental capacity.

Distribution of Work between the Criminal Trial Courts

This was reviewed by the James Committee, in 1976, whose report resulted in the Criminal Law Act 1977. They concluded that there were offences which were so serious in the public eye that they should always be triable on indictment "in order to signify the gravity with which society regards them." The 1977 Act redistributed work towards the magistrates' courts and there has been a further increase in the classification of offences as summary, in the Criminal Justice Act 1988 and other legislation. Lord Justice Auld performed a new review, in 2000. In October 2000 he noted that many respondents to his consultation had suggested introducing a mixed bench as a middle tier court to deal with the more serious triable either way cases. See his web-site at http://www.criminal-courts-review.org.uk.

Should There Be One Family Court?

Lord Chancellor Mackay saw the Children Act 1989 as a first step towards the creation of a family court, but no further progress has been made despite the fact that family courts exist in many other common law countries.

ALTERNATIVES TO THE COURTS

This century, some major alternative forums to the courts have been established. Lawyers should be concerned to discover to what extent their growth in popularity is a reflection on the inadequacies of the court system.

Tribunals

What are tribunals and how do they compare with courts? Tribunals are too disparate to be described as a "system." Indeed, there are over 100 sets of tribunals. Their only cohesive element is that many are supervised by the Council on Tribunals. It deals with day-to-day complaints on tribunal functioning, occasionally inspects proceedings and is consulted on the formulation of new tribunal procedural rules.

Tribunals are highly specialised, each set dealing with only one area of the law. Many deal with disputes between the citizen and the state, *e.g.* over tax or state benefits and others adjudicate between private parties, *e.g.* employment tribunals.

Some tribunals form a nationwide network (*e.g.* national insurance tribunals), whilst others are a single, central unit. Some sets contain an internal appeal structure, *e.g.* on immigration and employment.

Why have over 100 sets of tribunals developed alongside, but outside, the court system? Most tribunals have been created by statute, in the twentieth century. As the welfare state grew, so machinery became necessary to adjudicate between citizen and state. The Labour and Liberal governments which developed state power also distrusted the conservative (Conservative) judiciary, so created tribunals to serve this purpose.

Despite their concern over this creeping bureaucracy, Conservatives never stemmed the growth of tribunals. The Franks Committee was established, to examine their concern, and reported, in 1957, that tribunals should be seen as performing a judicial, not an executive, function and they should be better regulated. Their report led to statutory regulation under the Tribunals and Inquiries Act 1958 (now 1992) and the creation of the Council on Tribunals. The Franks Committee identified four main sets of reasons for the popularity of tribunals:

(i) Cheapness (no formal buildings or judicial regalia, etc.).
(ii) Accessibility and speed.
(iii) Freedom from technicality.
(iv) Expert knowledge (of the panel, compared with a judge, who is a Jack-of-all-trades).

A new review, chaired by Sir Andrew Leggatt, will report in 2001. Responses to the Review appeared on its website in November 2000 (http.//www.tribunals-review.org.uk).

Arbitration

Arbitration is, nowadays, the commercial world's alternative to slow, expensive and inconvenient High Court litigation. It means the adjudication of a dispute, usually by an individual expert in the subject-matter involved, or a lawyer. Arbitration may arise in one of three ways:

1. By contract. The parties may have contracted together, in some context, *e.g.* shipping or insurance and, in a clause of their contract, they have agreed to refer any disputes arising under it to an arbitrator (who may be named in the contract). This is significant, not just because it is common trade practice (*e.g.* in standard form building contracts), but also because lay people are often, unwittingly, parties to an arbitration clause. For instance, almost all insurance policies contain, in the small print, a clause stating that any dispute over a claim will first be referred to an arbitrator, before any court claim may be made. Where one of the parties tries to ignore such a clause, the court in which he makes his claim may order a "stay" (a stop) of proceedings so that the matter may be referred to arbitration.

2. By reference from the court. A judge in the Commercial Court may refer a dispute to an arbitrator.

3. By statute. The rise of arbitration occurred in the late nineteenth century when trade associations wished to have their disputes settled by experts in their trade. London is an international arbitration centre, dealing with 70 to 80 per cent of the world's maritime arbitrations. The popularity of arbitration now rests on expertise, privacy and finality. Some arbitrations are expensive and fraught with delay.

Small Claims

In the early 1970s the Consumers' Association and others criticised the county court system for being so cumbersome and expensive as to deter small claimants. Often costs were much higher than the amount claimed. In 1973, the small claims procedure was established in the county courts for claims under £100. Procedure is informal but not meant to be a complete departure from the adversarial model. Legal representation is allowed.

The Civil Justice Review 1988 recommended the automatic small claims procedure be extended to £1,000 (now £5,000) that "small claims" be referred to as such and have their own body of rules and that registrars (now district judges) hearing them should adopt an interventionist role, dispensing with formal rules of evidence and procedure and assuming control of evidence, thus clarifying that their role should be more inquisitorial than in the normal English court. Accordingly, the C.L.S.A. 1990, s.6 clarifies that rules may provide for this. Small claims are referred to again in the section on civil procedure.

Alternative Dispute Resolution (A.D.R.)

This is the fashionable development of the 1990s. Many British lawyers, most notably the previous and present Lord Chancellors, are taking an active interest in this American import, as a means of avoiding the public and private expense and the private pain of litigation. Many bodies are keen to extend the use of A.D.R. and, since the mid-1990s, civil advocates have been required to inform their clients of A.D.R.

There are three main categories: *mediation, conciliation* and *arbitration* (above). Schemes may be private or court-linked.

Mediation is the least formal. The parties voluntarily refer their dispute to an independent third party who will discuss the issues with both sides, normally in separate rooms and, by acting as a "go-between," she will assist them to discuss and negotiate areas of conflict and identify and settle certain issues. The best known of such schemes are those offered to family disputants. Thousands of people, notably solicitors, were trained as mediators to satisfy the requirements of the Family Law Act 1996. Divorcing couples were directed to meet a mediator but this part of the Act was abandoned in 1999, when pilots showed that only 7 per cent were diverted into mediation. Mediation is still available, however.

Conciliation lies midway between informal mediation and formal arbitration. The process is very similar to mediation but the third party may offer a non-binding opinion which *may* lead to a settlement.

Arbitration is the most formal (and established) type of A.D.R. (see above). It may be the last resort where conciliation fails. In certain schemes, a conciliator may transform into an arbitrator, where necessary, and pronounce a binding decision. The Woolf Report and civil procedure reforms (1999) emphasised A.D.R. For discussion see below.

2. SOURCES

DOMESTIC LEGISLATION

Whilst most principles of English law are derived from common law and equity, most details are now contained in statute law, *i.e.* Acts of Parliament and delegated legislation.

Acts of Parliament

E.C. lawyers would argue that it is no longer a constitutional fundamental that Parliament is sovereign, in that it can legislate whatever it sees fit. Because of the doctrine of subsidiarity, member states can only legislate on matters not covered by the Treaty of Rome. Acts which run counter to E.C. law run the danger of being suspended or declared invalid (*Factortame* (1991), see below). Provided an Act has been passed by both Houses, received royal assent and enrolled on to the parliamentary roll, it cannot be questioned by the courts. An exception to this is where the House of Lords refuses to pass a Bill. Under the Parliament Acts 1911, 1929, it may be overridden and passed by the Commons only (*e.g.* Sexual Offences Amendment Act 2000, which legalised homosexual acts at the age of 16). Parliament cannot be bound by its predecessors or bind its successors.

Functions of Acts.

1. Revision of substantive rules of law. The formation of the Law Commission in 1965 has helped keep the law under review and the modernisation and simplification of the law has sometimes been prompted by its reports or those of the Criminal Law Revision Committee or ad hoc Royal Commissions or committees.

2. Consolidation of enactments. Where law has evolved piecemeal, a single replacement Act of Parliament can be passed without debate.

3. Codification. The enacting of rules of common law.

4. Collection of revenue. The annual Finance Act implements the budget.

5. Social legislation. This broad category covers the many facets of the Government's running of the country and organisation of society. It is often the subject of party political differences.

Forms of Acts. Distinguish between (the more common) *public Acts* which are of general effect and *private Acts*, which deal with personal or local matters. Procedure differs.

Distinguish between *Government Bills*, the vast majority, *private bills, hybrid bills* and *private members' Bills*, promoted by M.P.s or peers, selected by ballot. Matters of conscience (*e.g.* abortion) are often left by the Government to be dealt with in this way.

Validity of Acts. Parliamentary sovereignty precludes the courts' questioning Acts of Parliament where there is no conflict with E.C. law and there is no written constitution against which the courts could test their constitutionality, as does the Supreme Court in the United States. The Human Rights Act 1998 permits a judge to make a declaration of incompatibility, where he finds an Act to conflict with the European Convention on Human Rights. This can only be done in the High Court and above. This will trigger a special section 11 fast-track Parliamentary procedure to amend the offending Act.

EUROPEAN COMMUNITIES LEGISLATION

Sources

The European Communities Act (E.C.A.) 1972 provides that any United Kingdom enactment has effect subject to existing "enforceable community rights" so, by implication, parliamentary sovereignty is limited to passing legislation which does not conflict.

Community Treaties established the European Community

and are its primary source of law. They are binding on the E.U. institutions and Member States and, in certain circumstances, may create individual rights enforceable in national courts. The fundamental Treaty is the Treaty of Rome 1957.

Article 249 of the E.C. Treaty sets out the following secondary legislative provisions:

1. Regulations have general, binding and direct applicability in all Member States.

2. Directives are binding, as to results to be achieved, upon each Member State to whom they are addressed, but leave form and methods to each Member State.

3. Decisions are binding on those to whom they are addressed.

Applicability and Enforcement

Distinguish between *direct applicability* and *direct effect.* The former concept refers to the fact that all Treaty Articles and all Regulations immediately become part of the law of each Member State. The latter concept is the vehicle through which individuals may assert that, under Community legislation, they have rights which the ECJ will protect and upon which they can rely in national courts.

The question as to whether a piece of legislation has direct effect is determined thus:

(a) Treaty Articles. In the *Van Gend en Loos* case (1963), the plaintiffs needed to know if they could rely on old Article 12 of the E.C. Treaty to ignore the Dutch government's increase of import duty. The ECJ, on a reference from the Dutch tribunal, held they could. The Article created individual enforceable rights because:

(i) It was clear and
(ii) it was unconditional.
(iii) Its implementation required no further legislation in Member States so that Member States were not left with any real discretion.

These tests have been applied to test the *direct effectiveness* of Treaty provisions, Regulations and Directives.

(b) Regulations. These have immediate applicability, as part of the law of each Member State. There is no need for further legislation to implement them and they are binding in their entirety and, like Treaty Articles, can be directly effective according to the above criteria.

(c) Directives. Nevertheless, directives may also have an *indirect effect* in that national law may have to be reinterpreted to conform to them. The *Marleasing* case (1990, ECJ) held that national courts are bound by Article 5 (now 10) EEC to reconcile all national law, pre- or post-dating a directive, in conformity with it. This development has mitigated the results of horizontal direct effect. In *Francovich and Bonifaci v. Italian Republic* (ECJ, 1991), the ECJ decided that an individual could sue the state directly where he had suffered loss as a result of non-implementation of a directive by the Member State.

(d) Decisions. The ECJ has held that these may create individual rights which domestic courts must protect. They have direct applicability and may have direct effect.

Supremacy of Community Law

Under Community law, that law takes precedence over any earlier or later domestic law. In *Costa v. E.N.E.L.* (1964), the Italian government submitted that its national courts were obliged to follow domestic law which conflicted with prior Community law. The ECJ ruled that, in creating a Community with its own legal capacity, "the member states have limited their sovereign rights, albeit within limited fields, and have thus created a body of law which binds both their nationals and themselves."

E.C.A. 1972, s.2 gives effect to Community law in the United Kingdom. Section 3(1) directs the United Kingdom courts to have regard to E.C. law. This includes the principle of supremacy. Where it appears to the English courts that there is inadvertently conflicting English legislation, they will endeavour to give effect to Community law.

The *Factortame* cases of 1990–1991 (on Spanish fishing in United Kingdom waters) illustrate the power and significance of Community law. In 1990, on a reference for a preliminary ruling from the House of Lords, the ECJ opined that a United Kingdom court could suspend the application of any Act of Parliament on the grounds of its alleged incompatibility with E.C. law and that Community law gave the national court the power to grant such interim relief, even though no such power existed in national law. Acting on this reference, the House confirmed that an interim injunction could be granted against the Crown, in such exceptional circumstances, to restrain it from enforcing an Act which, prima facie, contravened E.C. law. The novelty here is the use of an injunction against the Crown since this is, otherwise, impossible.

Subsequently, in 1991, the ECJ indeed ruled that part of the Merchant Shipping Act 1988 ran contrary to the E.C. Treaty. The concept of an Act of Parliament's being declared not to be in conformity with E.C. law came as no news to E.C. lawyers in the United Kingdom, who were swift to point out that we gave up part of our sovereignty in the 1972 Act but Press reaction was jingoistic and scandalised. Present law students cannot afford to be so insular.

STATUTORY INTERPRETATION

The Need for Interpretation

Interpretation of statutes is necessary because Parliament can only be expected to provide a broad legal framework. It is neither practical nor possible to expect a statute to spell out its effect in every set of circumstances, however obscure or complex, to which it will be required to apply. As the meaning of language is, in some instances, in the eye of the beholder, statutory interpretation is an inherently subjective art.

Furthermore, a draft Bill may be altered or added to by Parliament with minimal time for considering any problems of interpretation and it has long been a complaint of parliamentarians and critics alike that the legislative timetable does not allow for this.

Bennion, in his book, *Statute Law*, identified several factors which can cause doubt as to statutory meaning:

1. Ellipsis. This means the deliberate omission of words the draftsman thinks are implied. This causes no problem provided all the statute's readers realise what is implied.

2. Broad terms. The draftsman uses generic terms, again, deliberately, leaving the decision as to what falls into that category to the judge or statute user. For example, does the word "vehicle" cover a child's tricycle and a donkey cart?

3. Politic uncertainty. Ambiguous words may be used deliberately, where a provision is politically controversial or the government lacks clear intent.

4. Unforeseeable developments. Where novel circumstances arise after the passing of an Act.

5. Miscellaneous drafting errors. This includes accidental ambiguity and even printing errors.

Traditional "Rules" of Statutory Interpretation

The judges do not employ strict rules of interpretation but common approaches have been identified and labelled as such. To a certain extent, judges select which "rule" to use in accordance with the result they seek to achieve in the case before them. Quite often, judges purport, in doing this, to be seeking the "will" or "intention" of Parliament, as if a Parliament of over 600 M.P.s and over 400 regular attenders in the Lords could be said to have a common and identifiable "will." Other judges more blatantly admit, as did Lord Denning, "we fill in the gaps."

1. The Literal Rule. This simple approach involves giving words their ordinary, plain, natural meaning. One might think this such an obvious and straightforward activity it hardly merited being elevated to a "rule" of judicial behaviour but it was a trend of the eighteenth and nineteenth centuries, much stricter than the "mischief rule" (see below), which it supplanted. Some applications of the rule produce absurdity. For example, in *I.R.C. v. Hinchy* (1960), the House of Lords interpreted section 25(3) of the Income Tax Act 1952 which penalised those providing incorrect tax returns with a forfeit of "treble the tax which he ought to be charged under this Act." Although Parliament presumably intended a penalty of treble the unpaid tax, as the interpretation was rectified by immediate legislation, the House, nevertheless, held that a literal interpretation required the respondent to pay treble the whole amount of tax payable by him that year.

2. The Golden Rule. Rather than sanction an absurdity by the application of "the literal rule," judges may apply "the golden rule," permitting themselves to depart from giving words their "ordinary natural meaning." At its simplest, it states that, if words have more than one meaning, the least absurd is to be applied. The "rule" becomes more controversial in its wider sense, that is, that an absurdity must be avoided even if it results from the *only* interpretation. Some judges will take the pragmatic approach of "reinterpreting" the statute with the aim of reaching a common sense meaning, whereas others think this is no business of the judge.

3. The Mischief Rule. This rule is commonly described as the last judicial approach, if the first two "rules" fail to assist interpretation. It is much wider than the other "rules" and concentrates on determining the meaning of words by discovering the aim of the statute: the "mischief" at which the statute was directed.

Under the contextual approach, described below, the aim of the statute is considered as part of the context of the words being interpreted. Many modern judges take this approach from the outset.

The Contextual Approach

Sir Rupert Cross in *Statutory Interpretation* described, in a more sophisticated manner, the judicial approach to statutory interpretation.

Considering the context. In giving words their ordinary or technical meaning or in delimiting broad terms, the judge must take them in their general context of the statute, and in the statute's external context. According to *Att.-Gen. v. Prince Ernest Augustus of Hanover* (HL 1957, "the *Hanover* case") this includes the rest of the statute, the preamble, including the existing state of the law and the factual context, *i.e.* the mischief the statute was intended to remedy. The statute must be read as a whole.

Some judges refer to "a purposive approach," aiming to promote the general legislative purpose of a statute, to avoid, for example, ambiguities which would defeat the purpose of the statute but this can only be done where judges can determine this from internal or external aids to interpretation (see below) and where such an approach is not defeated by presumptions of interpretation.

Modifying statutory language to avoid unreasonableness. Under this approach, the judge may read in words which are necessarily implied and he has a limited power to add to, alter or ignore statutory words, to prevent a provision from being unintelligible, absurd, unreasonable, unworkable or totally irreconcilable with the rest of the statute. According to case law, this approach should only rarely be necessary if, for example, there is a mistake in drafting leading to an anomaly. There are a number of cases where the words "and" and "or" have been interchanged, to make sense of the statute.

Resorting to Presumptions and Aids to Construction

Internal aids to interpretation. Judges commonly say that statutes "must be read as a whole." This means that the first resort in interpretation may be found in the wording of the statute itself.

(i) *Other enacting words.* Another section may provide a clue to interpretation and there is often an interpretation section. For example, the Access to Justice Act 1999 defines such phrases as "criminal proceedings".

(ii) *Long title.* This sets out the aims of the Act. It can be as short as two lines, if the Act has one topic, as in the Legal Aid Act, or as long as a page, in a statute with diverse aims, such as the Criminal Justice Act 1988.

(iii) *Preamble.* Modern Acts may not have preambles but some, such as the Courts and Legal Services Act, set out their purpose in a section. The preamble cannot prevail over clear enacting words.

(iv) *Short title.*

(v) *Headings, side notes and punctuation.* Although not voted on by Parliament, these are acceptable aids.

Rules of Language

(i) *Ejusdem generis.* A general word following a list of particular ones will normally be construed as restricted in scope to applying to things or persons of the same class (*genus*) as those listed; *e.g.* in *Powell v. Kempton Park Race-*

course Co. (HL 1899) it had to be decided whether "house, office, room or other place" included Tattersall's ring at the racecourse. It was held not to be included because "house, office, room" created a *genus* of indoor places so an outdoor racecourse could not fall within an "other place."

(ii) *Noscitur a sociis*. This really means a word is to be construed as being similar to the rest of the objects in a list.

(iii) *Expressio unius exclusio alterus* means that a specified member of a class impliedly excludes other members. For example, the inclusion of "coal mines" in this list: "lands, houses, tithes and coal mines" has been held to impliedly exclude other mines.

External Aids

(i) Historical setting of the statute.
(ii) Dictionaries and textbooks.
(iii) Past practice.
(iv) Related statutes.
(v) Previous statutes. Consolidating statutes are presumed not to alter the law but clear language may rebut this.
(vi) Subordinate legislation.
(vii) Government publications (with certain qualifications), *e.g.* Royal Commission or Law Commission reports, Government White Papers.
(viii) Treaties and international conventions such as the Treaty of Rome and the European Convention on Human Rights.
(ix) Parliamentary materials. Until 1993, judges declined to refer to *Hansard* but in *Pepper v. Hart* (HL, 1993) the House of Lords held that this rule should be relaxed where legislation was ambiguous or obscure or the literal meaning led to an absurdity and, in identifying the true intention of the legislature, judges could be assisted by clear statements by the Bill's promoter.

Presumptions

(i) General principles. such as the principles of natural justice and the principle that no one should be allowed to profit from their own crime. These override even the clearest language.

(ii) Presumptions ousted by clear words. These are general principles of construction where Parliament must spell out in clear words any intention to avoid the following presumptions:

(a) against ousting the jurisdiction of the courts. The judges guard their own powers jealously and even some of the clearest "ouster" clauses have been held not to preclude judicial review;

(b) against interference with vested rights and that property cannot be taken away without compensation;

(c) against unduly penalising the citizen;

(d) against retrospectiveness;

(e) that statutes do not bind the Crown so that a very common inclusion in an Act is a section specifically binding the Crown (*e.g.* the Royal Family are not exempted from liability for traffic offences); and

(f) that Parliament does not intend to contravene the United Kingdom's international (Treaty) obligations or the European Convention on Human Rights.

The Interpretation of E.C. Law

The most important key to interpretation of Community law is the approach of the European Court of Justice (ECJ). The ECJ is more concerned with examining purpose and context than wording.

The Treaties are drafted in general terms, leaving it to the E.C. institutions, through secondary legislation, to fill in the details. The ECJ can review the legality of acts and omissions of the E.C. institutions.

The ECJ takes a dynamic approach in favour of the aims of the Community and the supremacy of E.C. law over national law, for example giving direct effect to directives. The ECJ employs a "rule of effectiveness" which means that preference should be given to the construction which gives a rule its fullest effect and it takes a contextual approach, referring to the general scheme of the Treaty or other Treaty provisions.

Exceptions to E.C. rules and Treaty obligations are restrictively interpreted, for example the principle of free movement of workers is limited by public policy, public security and public health and these limitations are strictly construed.

The ECJ refers to "general principles of law," common to all

Member States, derived from national law and, now, the principles laid down by the European Court of Human Rights, which can be employed in the interpretation of Treaty provisions but which cannot override them. These principles include such things as proportionality, *audi alteram partem*, equality and legal certainty. The general principles of law are now an important source of E.C. law and are used to interpret E.C. treaties and when examining national law for conformity with the treaties, as well as being almost a free standing source of law.

PRECEDENT

Significance

The primary hallmark of substantive law in the English legal system is that so much of it is a creation of the judiciary, through the application and development of case law and precedent. For example, the bulk of the law of tort and contract, as well as important crimes such as murder and common assault are a product of this system and not of Parliament. This distinguishes the English legal system from the codified systems of Europe and elsewhere. Under the system of binding precedent or *stare decisis* (to stand by previous decisions), inferior courts are bound to apply the legal principles set down by superior courts in earlier cases. This provides consistency and predictability and obviously depends on a system of law reporting.

The part of a case which forms the binding precedent is:

    (a) a statement of law (as opposed to fact);
    (b) which forms part of the *ratio decidendi* (reason for the decision); and
    (c) in a court whose decisions are binding.

The *Ratio Decidendi*

The *ratio decidendi* (plural, *rationes decidendi*) has been defined by Sir Rupert Cross, in his seminal work, *Precedent in English Law*, thus: "any rule of law expressly or impliedly treated by the judge as a necessary step in reaching his conclusion, having regard to the line of reasoning adopted by him, or a necessary part of his direction to the jury."

The *ratio decidendi* (*ratio*) must be distinguished from an *obiter dictum* (plural *dicta*) which is a statement of law not necessary for the decision in the case.

A judge may decline or find it difficult to apply the *ratio decidendi* of a previous decision because:

(1) he does not agree with it and has managed to find discrepancies in the instant case which allow him to distinguish it from the precedent; or

(2) no statements of principle appear in the precedent; or

(3) the *ratio* is difficult to extrapolate because different sets of reasoning have been used to found one decision, *e.g.* in House of Lords cases where there appear to be up to five *rationes decidendi* (*e.g. Hyam v. D.P.P.* (1974); *Boys v. Chaplin* (1968)).

Such decisions may be of some academic entertainment but can be a nightmare for practising lawyers and judges of the lower courts and do nothing to enhance certainty and predictability in the law.

The Function of the Court Hierarchy in the System of Precedent

The European Court of Justice and the European Court of Human Rights. Under section 3(1) of the European Communities Act 1972, decisions of this court are binding in matters of Community law, on all courts up to and including the House of Lords. Under s.2 of the Human Rights Act 1998, all courts must "take into account" the case law of the European Court of Human Rights, the Commission and Committee of Ministers when determining whether a Convention right has been breached.

The House of Lords. Decisions of the House of Lords are binding on all the courts below it and, until 1966, were binding on later decisions of the House itself. In 1966, however, the Lords of Appeal announced that they no longer intended to be bound by their previous decisions. This new, self-conferred power was intended to be used sparingly, however, to cater for revisions in law necessitated by changing social circumstances. It was such a change in societal attitudes which, arguably, led to the first application of the new power in *British Railways Board v. Herrington* (HL 1972), strengthening tortious protection for child trespassers, when the harsh precedent of *Addie v. Dumbreck* (HL 1929) was overturned. Since then, the House has used this power or consciously declined to use it, on a number of occasions.

The Court of Appeal (Civil Division). The Court of Appeal is bound by House of Lords decisions and its decisions are binding on all those courts below it.

Young v. Bristol Aeroplane Co. Ltd (1944). In this case, the Court of Appeal held itself to be bound by its own previous decisions, with three exceptions, listed (a) to (c) below.

(a) Decisions given *per incuriam* (means: through want of care). This refers to decisions made in ignorance or forgetfulness of some statutory provision or some binding precedent, notably because it has not been brought to the court's attention.
(b) Conflicting decisions of the Court of Appeal. There is no consensus on which of two conflicting decisions, the earlier or the later, should be followed.
(c) Decisions impliedly overruled by the House of Lords.

Later case law added the following exception:

(d) Decisions on interlocutory appeals, *i.e.* decisions taken by a Court of Appeal of only two judges.

Smith & Bailey in *The Modern English Legal System*, list, in addition, the following possible exceptions to *Young v. Bristol Aeroplane*:

(e) Inconsistency with an earlier House of Lords decision: the House of Lords decision is binding.
(f) Inconsistency with a Privy Council decision. This, however, is a dubious creation of Lord Denning M.R.

The House of Lords in *Davis v. Johnson* (1979) reaffirmed the rule that, other than in these cases, the Court of Appeal is bound by its own previous decisions. (See also *Rickards v. Rickards* (CA 1989).)

The Court of Appeal (Criminal Division). This division is bound by the House of Lords, by itself and by its historical predecessors, unless it is a Court of Appeal decision falling into one of the exceptions in *Young v. Bristol Aeroplane.* Additionally, it was laid down in *R. v. Newsome, R. v. Brown* (CA 1970) that a "full court" of five Lords Justices has the power to overrule a previous decision of a court of three.

It is uncertain whether the two divisions of the Court of Appeal bind each other but certainly, in some instances, they have manifested an intention not to be so bound, for example, in their conflicting approach towards the constitutionality of jury vetting in *R. v. Crown Court at Sheffield, ex p. Brownlow* (1980) and *R. v. Mason* (1980).

The High Court. The High Court is, of course, bound by the Court of Appeal and the House of Lords but is not bound by other High Court decisions.

Divisional Courts of the High Court. Divisional Courts, within each division of the High Court are, when exercising their appellate function, binding on their successors and amenable to the principles in *Young v. Bristol Aeroplane* but not when exercising their judicial review function (*R. v. G. Manchester Coroner, ex p. Tal* (1984)).

The Crown Court, magistrates' courts and county court. These decisions are seldom reported and are not binding on any court.

Tribunals. Where a tribunal system has an internal appeal structure, as with employment tribunals and the Employment Appeal Tribunal, the decisions of the appellate tribunal are binding but tribunals are not binding on each other. Indeed, tribunals are not meant to develop systems of precedent. That is one of the features distinguishing them from courts, even though some tribunals enjoy more than one series of reports of their cases and some tribunals look very much more like courts than others.

Persuasive Precedents

Precedents which are not binding may be taken as persuasive and, indeed, have played a significant part in assisting judicial creativity where there are gaps in the law, a classic example being the development of liability for negligent misstatements resulting in pure economic loss, from an *obiter* statement of the House of Lords. The following precedents are persuasive:

1. *Obiter dicta* of the House of Lords.
2. Decisions of the Privy Council.
3. Decisions from other common law jurisdictions.
4. Textbooks.
5. Judgments of parallel courts, where these are not binding, for example, the High Court.

Law Reporting

Any system of precedent could not function without an efficient system of law reporting. It started privately but somewhat randomly in the thirteenth century but was only put on a formal and more systematic basis in 1870 with the creation of the Incorporated Council of Law Reporting for England and Wales. This body publishes the official *Law Reports* whose contents are preferable in authority to other series of reports, as they are checked and amended by the judges. Nevertheless, they are often practically inconvenient as other reports such as *The Weekly Law Reports* are published so much more quickly.

Databases of both statute and case law, such as *Lexis*, have revolutionised law reporting and the advocate's ability to rely on a broad span of pertinent authorities as they include all decisions, whether reported elsewhere or not.

3. PERSONNEL

LAWYERS

The chief feature of the English legal profession is that it is divided into two sections, solicitors and barristers. The two sides were, traditionally, characterised by their monopolies. The Bar had a monopoly over rights of audience in the higher courts and solicitors have a monopoly over initial contact with most clients. Until recently, solicitors' best-known monopoly was conveyancing. These monopolies have been considerably eroded in the 1980s and 90s and the legal profession has been in a state of flux since it was the subject of scrutiny by the Royal Commission on Legal Services (R.C.L.S.) 1976–1979.

Solicitors

Structure and organisation. On July 31, 1999, there were 100,957 solicitors on the Roll, 79,503 of whom had practising certificates, distributed amongst over 8,561 firms in England and Wales. *The Law Society* is the professional governing body of solicitors, regulating their training, discipline and standards of professional conduct and it is also their trade union.

Complaints and discipline procedure. Since May 1991, all solicitors' firms must have an in-house complaint-handling procedure. Otherwise complaints are processed by the Society itself. The R.C.L.S. heavily criticised the Law Society's handling of complaints. The Law Society reorganised their complaints mechanism and, in 1996, created the Office for the Supervision of Solicitors but there is repeated criticism of the Office's inability to handle its large backlog of complaints, especially by the Legal Services Ombudsman who said in 1999 that it was spiralling out of control. Two pieces of research had condemned the Office's inefficiency and in 2000 the Director General of Fair Trading gave the Law Society a "final warning" to put their house in order. In the Access to Justice Act 1999, the Lord Chancellor was empowered to appoint a Legal Services Commissioner if the Law Society does not correct the problem. Complaints are handled thus: Complainants may first seek advice from a telephone helpline. Most are referred to a conciliator or to a mediator. At least 30 per cent of complaints are resolved in this way. If conciliation fails, the matter is dealt with formally, with written reports. An assistant director may decide what action to take, with a right of appeal. The O.S.S. has a broad range of powers, including: inspecting the solicitor's accounts; taking control of her files or accounts; or ordering compensation or remission of fees.

It may also prosecute the solicitor before the *Solicitors Disciplinary Tribunal*, which can reprimand, fine, suspend the solicitor or order her to be struck off.

Appeal lies to the High Court or Master of the Rolls. Any complainant not satisfied with the handling of a complaint by the Bureau may complain to the *Legal Services Ombudsman*.

Sex discrimination. The proportion of solicitors holding practising certificates who are women is 35.1 per cent. This reflects a steady growth but it by no means reflects the growth in the proportion of law graduates who are women (around 51 per cent), or women as new trainee solicitors (56.4 per cent), or women of those newly admitted (52.6 per cent).

The Law Society's *Annual Statistical Report* 1997 which provides these statistics also demonstrates how few women are partners. 85.5 per cent of men with 10–19 years' experience are partners compared with only 60.5 per cent of women, although the proportion of solicitors, including partners, who are women, is growing.

A 1997 salary survey revealed that female solicitors earn significantly less then their male counterparts, even when all relevant factors, such as experience, are comparable.

Race discrimination. The R.C.L.S., in 1979, found discrimination in both sides of the profession. It deprecated the formation of firms of solicitors and chambers composed solely of members of ethnic minorities. If black-only firms served black clients and briefed black barristers then the public would come to think such discrimination was reflected in the administration of justice itself.

The Law Society in 1986 belatedly established an ethnic monitoring scheme and a Race Relations Committee to examine complaints of discrimination, consider relevant statistics and work to "enhance awareness in the profession." In 1999, about 5.5 per cent of solicitors with practising certificates were from ethnic minorities, compared with 5.2 per cent of the economically active population. 19.4 per cent of students enrolling with the Law Society are non-white but the biggest problem minorities face is in entering the profession and progressing to partnerships within it. A Law Society survey in 1999 showed minorities and women experience difficulty in securing traineeships.

Barristers

Structure and organisation. On October 1, 2000 there were 10,132 practising barristers, distributed between 604 sets of chambers, of which 311 were in London, or working as sole practitioners (197). The Bar has grown considerably since 1960, when there were only 1,919 practising barristers.

The General Council of the Bar and of the Inns of Court (known as *"the Bar Council"*) is the professional governing body of the Bar. It comprises elected barristers. The Bar Council performs similar professional functions to the Law Society. In addition, the six court circuits have their own Bar Associations, as do specialist barristers.

Further, there are four *Inns of Court*, Gray's Inn, Lincoln's Inn, Inner Temple and Middle Temple and each barrister must belong to an Inn of Court. The Inns, in their (fascinating) history had a collegiate function. Nowadays they own and administer much of the property in which barristers rent accommodation for their chambers (offices).

The Council of Legal Education regulates and provides training.

Complaints and discipline. In 1997, the Bar established a formal system for dealing with complaints, supervised by a Complaints Commissioner. He may award up to £2,000 compensation, with the ultimate sanction being an appearance before the Disciplinary Tribunal, which may reprimand, suspend, disbar and order repayment of fees.

In 2000 in *Arthur J.S. Hall (a firm) v. Simons* the House of Lords held that barristers and other advocates (including solicitors) could be sued for negligence in their conduct of civil and criminal proceedings. This reversed the old rule in *Rondel v. Worsely* (1969). This has led to calls for the Bar Council to permit barristers to sue for their fees. The Courts and Legal Services Act 1990 permits this and allows barristers to contract for their services. Historically, they did not do so because it was thought unseemly in a gentleman's profession.

Archaic practising arrangements

1. Chambers. Until 1990 every practising barrister had to rent a "tenancy" (really a sub-tenancy) in a "set" of chambers and until the 1980s most London Chambers had to be within the Inns of Court in accordance with an unwritten rule. The growth of the Bar since the 1960s led to chronic overcrowding in the Inns of Court and by 1990 the Bar Council resolved to abandon all restrictions on the setting up of new chambers. Barristers of three years' call may now practise independently (for example from home).

2. The clerk. Most sets of chambers have one chief clerk, or practice manager, and several juniors. All barristers in chambers must obtain their work and negotiate for fees through the medium of the clerk. Barristers need clerks as office and business managers and agents.

3. The hierarchy. The top 10 per cent or so of barristers are called Queen's Counsel, more commonly called "silks," as they are entitled to wear a silk gown instead of the ordinary stuff gown. All other barristers, however elderly, are known as junior barristers or pupils (see below). Q.C.s take the most serious cases and charge high fees.

Q.C.s are appointed by the Crown on the recommendation of the Lord Chancellor. Junior barristers apply to "take silk." Most apply because they wish to specialise in advocacy and have built up a workload and reputation that justifies hiving off some of their preparatory work to junior counsel. There used to be a rule called the Two Counsel Rule whereby a Q.C. had to pay a junior to appear with him in court. This was abolished in 1977, following criticism by the Monopolies and Mergers Commission, but it is still widely followed, in practice. The practice has been the subject of repeated criticism and scrutiny and in 2000, the Lord Chancellor further restricted the use of silk or more than one advocate, in legally aided Crown Court cases. The Law Society is campaigning to abolish the rank of Q.C.

4. Partnerships. Barristers stand or fall by their own individual skills (and health). They are not allowed to form partnerships except if practising overseas.

5. Unpaid pupillage. Barristers are qualified as soon as they are "called" on passing the Bar Finals but, if they wish to offer legal services, they must do a one-year apprenticeship, called pupillage. In this, they watch their "pupil-master" in court and are supposed to be trained by him but most of them do some work for him, and are not paid for it. They can earn fees by taking cases on their own account, in their second six months but having to support themselves in their first six was one of the factors which made going to the Bar so expensive for those who did not have family or other financial backing to maintain them. The Bar has endeavoured to ease this problem by providing pupillage funding. A 2000 case determined that pupils are not entitled to the national minimum wage (*Edmonds v. Lawson*, CA).

6. Rules of etiquette and unwritten rules. These seem largely designed to mark out the Bar as an elite, relative to solicitors and clients. They also serve as a good tourist attraction. These are some of the best known:

(a) Barristers wear wigs in certain courts but Lord Mackay L.C. refused solicitor-advocates permission to do so.

(b) They use grovelling language to the bench, *e.g.* "may it please your Lordship . . .," "I humbly submit." Fellow barristers are referred to as "my learned friend," whereas solicitors are simply "my friend."

(c) There are strict rules of dress which require all to wear dark suits and women to look as much as possible like men. Most men wear a waistcoated suit and, under the wig and gown, this garb can be too hot in summer.

(d) Barristers are forbidden from interviewing their clients, other than in the presence of the solicitor.

Sex discrimination. The R.C.L.S. (1979) found that over 90 sets contained no women and some sets of chambers were prepared to admit to a "no women" policy. The proportion of women as practising barristers is nevertheless increasing (26 per cent on October 1, 1997) and, in 1990, the C.L.S.A., s.64 outlawed sex discrimination (see below).

Race discrimination. There have long been complaints by black barristers that racism is institutionalised at the Bar. The R.C.L.S. deprecated the concentration of ethnic minorities into "ghetto" chambers and 10 years later, a 1989 survey showed that half of all chambers had no ethnic minority tenants and 53 per cent of non-white barristers were concentrated in 16 sets of chambers.

The Bar established a Race Relations Committee in 1983. The C.L.S.A. 1990, s.64 illegalised sex and race discrimination by, or in relation to barristers, in terms of offers of pupillage, tenancies and the distribution of work by the clerk and the provision of it (by solicitors), etc.

Amid continuing and widespread allegations of discrimination, in 1991 the Bar Council adopted what *The Independent* described as "the most radical equal opportunities policy of any profession." It proposes that all sets should aim to have five per cent of their tenants from ethnic minorities and that public and private bodies should be encouraged to send five per cent of their legal work to ethnic minority barristers, with the Council publishing an ethnic minority directory to this end.

In 1993, the Council for Legal Education introduced a central selection Board to review its Bar vocational course selection procedures, as statistics showed white candidates were twice as likely to be admitted as non-whites. At the same time, the Barrow Committee investigated discrepancies between white and minority success rates in the Bar exams. It reported, in April 1994, that even after sophisticated analysis of prior educational achievement, ethnicity was a significant determinant of success, as were offers of a pupillage and achievement of scholarships, in all of which respects white candidates fare better. In 1994 the Commission for Racial Equality conducted a formal investigation into the C.L.E.

The Abolition of the Conveyancing Monopoly

Perhaps the best known professional monopoly was that of solicitors over property conveyancing. It was the main driving force of controversy behind the establishment of the R.C.L.S. Conveyancing had long been known as the "bread-and-butter" fee earner for solicitors. The public complaint was that the monopoly allowed overcharging. Solicitors defended themselves by saying the monopoly protected the public from charlatans.

The R.C.L.S. disappointed all critics by recommending in favour of the monopoly but in 1984, the Farrand Committee recommended a system of licensed conveyancers which was effected by the Administration of Justice Act 1985.

Lord Mackay produced new proposals for legislation regulating conveyancing in one of his famous 1989 pack of three *Green Papers* on reforming legal services. It was entitled *Conveyancing by Authorised Practitioners* (Cm. 572) and proposed to permit conveyancing by banks and building societies under a simplified framework.

The green paper denied solicitors' allegations that there would be a danger of conflicts of interest in "one-stop shopping" by house buyers obtaining their new home, conveyancing and mortgage under one roof, as lending institutions would only be permitted to do conveyancing by using employed solicitors or licensed conveyancers. Solicitors continued to argue that the public would be insufficiently protected and, worse, that the "unfair competition" from banks and building societies would extinguish most firms of high street solicitors, thus denying the public easy access to legal services.

There swiftly followed the Government's refined plans in the 1989 *White Paper*, entitled *Legal Services: A Framework For the Future* (Cm. 740). The end product, the C.L.S.A. 1990, ss.34–53, provides the regulatory machinery. *Section 17* sets out *the statutory objective and the general principle* of providing for new or better ways of providing legal services (including conveyancing services) and a wider choice of persons providing them. *Sections 34 and 35* establish *The Authorised Conveyancing Practitioners Board*, with the general duty to seek to develop competition in the provision of conveyancing services and to authorise conveyancing practitioners. *Section 43* requires the Board to set up a *conveyancing ombudsman scheme* to hear complaints about authorised practitioners.

Repercussions of the Abolition

1. Advertising. The ban on solicitors' advertising was relaxed, in the 1980s. Solicitors now advertise on radio, television and in newspapers.

2. Conveyancing costs fell, probably as a result of internal competition (the public habit of "shopping around" rather than remaining faithful to "the family solicitor"). By 1991 some firms started to form networks, preparing to offer attractive conveyancing packages to banks and building societies.

3. Property shops. Solicitors began selling houses, allowing the client to obtain estate agency and conveyancing services under one roof, but numbers of firms selling houses declined dramatically, with the recession, from 1989–1994. Solicitors' Property Centres were relaunched in the late 1990s.

4. A Legal Practice Directorate (now policy directorate) was established, in 1987, by the Law Society to identify areas where solicitors could expand their work. They emphasised potential new work in: advocacy; A.D.R.; financial services; the single European market; multinational partnerships; networking and specialising in personal injury work, disaster litigation, social security, etc.

Abolition of the Probate and Litigation Monopolies

As well as enjoying a monopoly over conveyancing, for most of the twentieth century, solicitors have also held monopolies over *probate work* and the *conduct of litigation*, similarly protected by the Solicitors Act. C.L.S.A., s.28. permits appropriate "authorised bodies" (*i.e.* professional bodies, notably the Law Society) to grant the right to conduct litigation, in a broadly similar way to the granting of rights of audience. Sections 54 and 55 of the C.L.S.A. open up probate services to approved banks, building societies, insurance companies and legal executives.

Abolishing the Bar's Monopoly over Rights of Audience

Solicitors have long held a statutory right to appear in magistrates' courts, county courts and (in a very few localities), in the Crown Court. Barristers have enjoyed a customary monopoly, fixed by a committee of judges, over rights of audience in the High Court, the Court of Appeal and the House of Lords. Most significant in terms of the work it provided was their monopoly over the right to appear in most areas of the Crown Court.

In 1984, as an immediate response to the threat to its conveyancing monopoly, the Law Society launched a campaign for rights of audience in all higher courts.

This was just the latest in a long series of attacks made by solicitors on the Bar's monopoly. To the Bar's relief, the R.C.L.S. had, in 1979, rejected solicitors' arguments, concluding that such an extension would be against the public interest because:

(i) If solicitors were permitted rights of audience only in the Crown Court, this would destroy the livelihood of new junior barristers, who derived 50 per cent of their income from such work.

(ii) Jury advocacy involves special skills, only to be maintained with practice, which most solicitors could not spare the time to keep up.

(iii) Since it is up to the solicitor, under the present system, to select a barrister, he can make a more informed selection than the client could, left to choose amongst all advocates.

In 1986, in order to take the heat out of their dispute, the two sides of the profession established the Committee on the Future of The Legal Profession (The Marre Committee). It reported in

July 1988, recommending that solicitors should have extended rights of audience in the Crown Court and should be eligible for appointment as High Court judges.

Changes made by the Conservative government. It soon became clear that the Lord Chancellor, Lord Mackay, was keen to extend the Thatcherite approach to monopolies to the Bar's work. In 1989, he published his three *Green Papers* and his white paper, *Legal Services; A Framework for the Future*, making it clear that the Government view was that the best possible access to legal services was achieved by giving clients the widest possible choice within a free and efficient market. This philosophy was to be applied to the right to appear in court, in the same way as to conveyancing, probate, etc. (see above) and all legal services.

In the main Green Paper, *The Work and Organisation of the Legal Profession* (Cm. 570), the Government set out their views on advocacy. Our adversarial system meant that the court and the client were heavily reliant on the efficient and effective preparation and presentation of a case and the maintenance of high ethical standards. Rights of audience should be restricted to those who are properly trained, experienced and subject to codes of conduct. The basic premise was that satisfaction of those requirements should, alone, be the test for granting rights of audience, not whether an advocate happened to be a barrister or solicitor.

The white paper proposals on rights of audience were enacted in the Courts and Legal Services Act 1990. It provided that rights to appear could only be granted by the "appropriate authorised body" and made similar provision for the *right to conduct litigation*. The Lord Chancellor, the Director General of Fair Trading, the Advisory Committee and "designated judges," each had a role in authorising a new body. Barristers' and solicitors' existing audience rights were preserved and their governing bodies were accordingly deemed authorised bodies under the Act.

Repercussions of the Abolition. As with solicitors, the threat of having to compete for work in an open market had an important impact on the Bar. In some respects, it relaxed a number of its practice rules and has even had to acquaint itself with twenty-first century business practice and marketing methods, a real shock to the system for this pre-Dickensian profession:

1. Relaxing advertising rules. Sets of chambers, since 1991, list their members in national newspaper ads, and the Bar uses P.R. consultants.

2. Promoting new areas of work. For example marketing to those professions who may now access them directly, such as accountants, architects, banks, insurers and trade unions; promoting themselves as specialist advocates and merging chambers to provide stronger units.

3. Relaxing the chambers rule

4. Permitting direct access to non-practising, employed barristers by their employers' clients. This is important, since there are now nearly as many employed barristers as practising ones.

5. Paying pupils and reforming training.

6. Developing Bar Mark. A kitemarking system based on best practice.

Life after the Courts and Legal Services Act

By 2000, ten years after the Act came into force, nothing has happened. Licensed conveyancers did not destroy the solicitors' side of the profession, as solicitors of the 1970s shrieked it would, since, by 2000, there are still only 750 of them and over 100,000 solicitors. Most conveyancing is still done by solicitors.

Since the 1990 Act there have been arguments involving solicitors, the Bar, the judiciary and the Crown Prosecution Service over rights of audience. The Law Society can now authorise private practitioners as advocates but by 2000, there are only 1075, many of whom do not use their rights of audience. This is hardly likely to destroy the Bar as we know it and the Bar has doubled in size since 1983.

A Frustrated Labour Lord Chancellor, The Access to Justice Act 1999 and Rights of Audience

The present Lord Chancellor signalled his impatience by promoting the Access to Justice Act.

Sections 36–43 are some of the most provocative elements of the Act. They are headed *Rights of audience and rights to conduct litigation* and stem from the Chancellor's frustration at the lack of progress in opening up rights of audience, one of the stated aims of the Courts and Legal Services Act 1990. His June 1998 consultation paper, *Rights of Audience and Rights to Conduct Litigation in England and Wales* is a gem of colourful language and vituperation against the forces of inertia which have protected the Bar's restrictive practice, their monopoly over rights of audience in the higher courts. He portrays the Bar Council, his advisory committee (ACLEC) and the designated judges, as conspiring to clog the cogs in the clanking machinery of the 1990 Act, to stop other lawyers getting rights of audience.

Section 36 gives all barristers rights of audience in all courts and all solicitors rights of audience and rights to conduct litigation in all courts, subject only to rules prescribed by the Law Society.

Section 37 is very controversial and was vociferously opposed by the Bar. It prohibits restrictions on rights of audience for employed lawyers. This is a great victory for the Crown Prosecution Service, who may now send employed lawyers to appear in the Crown Court, and for employed solicitors. Lord Irvine told the "sorry saga" of their six year attempt to get audience rights, in graphic detail, in the consultation paper. They had ended up with virtually useless rights.

Section 39 makes audience rights portable from one profession to another so a barrister no longer loses higher court audience rights by becoming a solicitor or a member of the CPS. Section 40 makes the Bar Council and ILEX authorised bodies, empowered to grant rights to conduct litigation.

Section 42 imposes on all advocates and litigators a duty to the court and a duty to act in the interests of justice, formerly common law duties.

The Bar had opposed the granting of rights of audience to CPS lawyers on the ground that the interests of justice are better served by an advocate who is entirely independent and can represent the prosecution one day and the defence the next, with impartiality.

Section 35 abolishes ACLEC, which the L.C. criticised in his paper on rights of audience. He thought it had too many people, cost too much (£1 million p.a.) and had succeeded in obstructing rather than furthering the statutory objective of the Courts and Legal Services Act 1990, to open up competition in the provision of legal services. It is replaced with a small Legal Services Consultative Panel, appointed by the L.C., with "a duty of assisting in the maintenance and development of standards in the education, training and conduct of persons offering legal services by considering relevant issues in accordance with a programme of work approved by the Lord Chancellor and, where the Consultative Panel considers it appropriate to do so, making recommendations to him". They are obliged to advise the L.C. when he calls on them.

Fusion

The subject of fusion, *i.e.* whether the two sides of the legal profession should be fused into one, has been a topic of controversy for decades. Many commentators consider the Access to Justice Act 1999 will be a large step towards fusion.

Legal Education

Briefly, it is as follows, roughly in line with the recommendations of the Ormrod Committee on Legal Education (1971):

Barristers. All-graduate entry. Non-law graduates and mature students do a one-year Common Professional Examination (the academic stage), then they and law graduates do a one-year Bar Vocational Course. Students must dine 12 times at their Inn of Court. After this, successful candidates may be called to the Bar. All barristers, employed or independent, offering legal services must do one year of pupillage. During the first six months, pupils may not earn fees and this had led to hardship in the past. Recently the Bar has promoted a scheme whereby all pupils should be paid, either by their chambers or from a central fund. All barristers must undertake continuing education.

Solicitors. Non-law graduates and mature students do the C.P.E. or diploma in law. Then they and law graduates take the Legal Practice Course (one year). All must complete a two-year traineeship before being admitted. All solicitors must now undertake continuing education courses.

In 1996, the Lord Chancellor's Advisory Committee on Legal Education and Conduct produced a report suggesting a common 15–18 week training for both sides of the profession followed by a specialist 15–18 week course for solicitors (LPC) or barristers (BVC) and by in-service training as a pupil barrister or trainee solicitor.

JUDGES

The Heads of Division

The Lord Chancellor (Lord Irvine of Lairg L.C.) is the head of the judiciary, President of the Supreme Court and President of the Chancery Division. *If* he sits as a judge, he does so in the House of Lords or Privy Council. He effectively selects most judges and has overall responsibility for the court service, legal services, and the Law Commission. His executive position makes his role as head of the judiciary controversial. Although appointed by the monarch, he is effectively selected by the Prime Minister, is a member of the Government, and normally a Cabinet Minister so the incumbent changes when the Government changes. He is Speaker of the House of Lords. He thus holds important offices in all three organs of government: legislature, executive and judiciary.

The Lord Chief Justice of England (Lord Woolf L.C.J.) is President of the Court of Appeal (Criminal Division) and head of the Queen's Bench Division of the High Court.

The Master of the Rolls (Lord Phillips M.R.) is the President of the Court of Appeal (Civil Division).

The President of the Family Division (Dame Elizabeth Butler-Sloss P.) and the *Vice-Chancellor* (Sir Andrew Morritt) who is, effectively, head of the Chancery Division, are *ex officio* members of the Court of Appeal.

Independence

It is a constitutional fundamental that judges are independent, that is, beyond the influence of the executive, apolitical, incorruptible and unbiased. Rules and conventions support this:

1. Superior and circuit judges, but not recorders, are statute barred from being M.P.s.

2. Judicial peers (Lords of Appeal, Lord Chancellor and Heads of Division) refrain from participation in House of Lords political debates although they do speak on law reform.

3. Judges are disqualified, by common law, from dealing with cases in which they have an interest, proprietary or personal.

4. Judges are paid large salaries, supposedly to keep them above corruption, which are calculated by the Top Salaries Review Board and not subject to a vote in Parliament.

Regular use is made of judicial impartiality by appointing them to head inquiries into politically sensitive issues such as Lord Scarman's investigation into the Brixton Riots of 1981, Woolf L.J.'s inquiry into the 1990 prison riots and Sir Richard Scott's inquiry into the Conservative Government's illegal sales of arms to Iraq, reported in 1996.

Judicial Neutrality

Writers such as Griffith in *The Politics of The Judiciary* are, however, less concerned over the previously declared political allegiance of the judiciary than over their narrow political and social class backgrounds and socialisation at the Bar, consciously or unconsciously influencing judges, especially in political cases (*e.g.* in administrative law and in cases involving labour relations, civil liberties, students and immigrants, etc., Griffith and other critics traditionally argued that judges showed a significantly "right-wing" approach but this criticism could not be applied to judges of the 1990s and this decade, seen by the Conservatives and New Labour as a radical and outspoken nuisance).

Qualifications

The Courts and Legal Services Act 1990 reformed eligibility for appointment by basing it on rights of audience. Prior to the Act, solicitors of specified standing had been eligible for appointment up to the circuit bench and barristers for all appointments. This had been a source of controversy between the two sides of the profession, solicitors arguing that making them eligible for the High Court would widen the pool of able candidates.

Whilst the C.L.S.A. will ultimately respond to this criticism by making solicitors with rights of audience eligible, there is only one solicitor High Court judge, as of 2001 and the Act has been criticised, by the pressure group JUSTICE, in *The Judiciary in England and Wales*, 1992. Practice as an advocate, they argue, does not guarantee the qualities necessary for a good judge and "the strong combative or competitive streak present in many successful advocates is out of place on the bench."

Appointment and Selection

Perhaps the most spectacular breach of the doctrines of the separation of powers and judicial independence is the Lord Chancellor (see above). The selection of all judges is effectively in his gift or his and the Prime Minister's. Lord Chancellors have, occasionally, been accused of party political bias (*e.g.* Lord Halsbury last century) and governments are sometimes accused of rewarding their political supporters.

This selection method and criteria have not changed much since Lord Hailsham L.C., in 1985, described his method of selecting judges. He said he applied three principles:

(i) To appoint solely on merit.

(ii) That no single person's view on a candidate should be regarded as decisive.

(iii) That candidates should not be appointed to permanent posts until they had proved themselves in a part-time capacity, in an elaborate system of part-time deputy High Court judges and recorders, developed since 1971.

Senior staff gather factual information from the candidate and opinions from the judiciary and senior members of the profession, who know the candidate, in "consultations". These, and notes on interviews, are kept on file, the factual information being open to the candidate's inspection.

The convention was that barristers did not apply to be High Court judges but, since 1998, they may now apply. The Lord Chancellor reviews the field of choice, in consultation with the heads of division. (Lord Mackay announced he also consulted the head of the Bar.) It was necessary for candidates to apply to be circuit judges. The Conservative Lord Chancellor, Lord Mackay refused to change this consultation system. He explained it in some detail in *Judicial Appointments*, a booklet available free from the L.C.D. website, updated 1999.

The Law Society have argued that the present system of

appointment, with its reliance on the appointee's experience as an advocate and existing judges' personal recommendations to the Lord Chancellor, discriminates against women, ethnic minorities and solicitors in general, regardless of the Lord Chancellor's repeated assurances that he is keen to recruit more judges from these groups. Indeed, Lord Mackay expressed this as an open policy in *Judicial Appointments* and, in 1994, he announced new plans designed to encourage more women and ethnic minorities to apply. Nevertheless, in 1996–97 the Association of Women Barristers vociferously criticised the appointments system as being biased against women. They consider gender bias to be prevalent in court proceedings. In 1999, the Law Society, still very critical of this system, announced a boycott of the consultation process, which they call "secret soundings".

Groups such as JUSTICE have repeatedly criticised the system of appointment based on the say-so of one person, at that a member of the Government, the Lord Chancellor. This is an anachronism, they argue, stemming from the days when he knew all the candidates. They suggest a Judicial Appointments Commission, independent of the executive, of 13 people, 7 of them lay, which would appoint all judges and supervise their training, career development and standards of performance. Lord Mackay resisted this suggestion, insisting that appointments should still be made by the Lord Chancellor but in 1993 he announced a programme of reform for judicial appointments procedures. It emphasised forecasting and planning the need for judges; preparing job descriptions and particularising the qualities needed; introducing open advertising for judicial appointments below the High Court level (Lord Irvine extended this to High Court appointments); the progressive introduction of competitions for vacancies; further measures to encourage applications from women and ethnic minorities; a more structured basis for consultations with the judiciary and the profession and involving lay people (as advisers only) in the selection process. This plan was fully implemented by 1995. In 1997, the Labour Government announced plans for a Judicial Appointment Commission to draw up a shortlist of candidates for the L.C.'s consideration but retracted these plans, Lord Chancellor Irvine explaining that there was not the time to effect this reform.

In 1999, the Lord Chancellor asked Sir Leonard Peach to review the judicial appointments process. Lord Irvine revealed potential judges are continuously assessed by lawyers and judges for such qualities as humanity, courtesy and understanding of society. Peach's overall assessment of the current system of appointments is favourable. His terms of reference precluded his reviewing by whom appointments are made. He recommended the creation of a Judicial Appointments Commission, purely to investigate grievances and complaints and to audit appointment processes and policies and recommend changes to the Lord Chancellor. Its membership would closely resemble other country's commissions. For applicants of whom little is known, he recommended they nominate 3–6 consultees. The report recommended that advocacy no longer be an essential element in the selection process and Lord Irvine has accepted that. Peach proposes alternative methods of assessing suitability, such as one-day assessment centres and psychometric testing. He thinks more judges should be promoted from the lower ranks. (See report on L.C.D. website and critique by Malleson at (2000) 150 N.L.J. 8). The Law Society still calls the system an old boy network and demands an end to secret soundings. In October 2000, they published a report, *Broadening the Bench*, outlining their proposals for reform. A 1999 JUSTICE report called for the withdrawal of the Law Lords from their Parliamentary seats, arguing that the system breaches the European Convention on Human Rights.

Since 1999, the *Judicial Appointments Annual Report* appears on the website. There are now nine women in the High Court, including Lady Justice Butler-Sloss, President of the Family Division. Of all judicial appointments, 1998–99, 23.5 per cent were women and 5.4 per cent ethnic minority. The L.C. increased the statutory ceiling of High Court judges to 106 because of the Human Rights Act.

Promotion

There is no career judiciary in the English legal system. A circuit judge, for example, does not expect to be "promoted" to the High Court and so on. Career judiciaries are a common pattern elsewhere in Europe, where graduates may choose to train for the judiciary rather than practise and can expect eventual promotion and regrading in the same manner as the civil service. Their judges are consequently much younger, on average, than our judges. In 1992, JUSTICE repeated their 1972 suggestion of a structured judicial career path and the Labour Government has promised a "more rational training and career structure".

Social Background

Quite apart from the fact that our judiciary is almost exclusively white and male, much research and comment has been devoted to the narrow social background of the judiciary. The results of most of this are cited by Griffith, demonstrating that at least 75 per cent. of most judicial samples surveyed came from upper or upper middle class families, and attended public school and then Oxford or Cambridge. All surveys, such as that of the House of Commons Home Affairs Committee, in 1995, indicate that most judges are over 60 years old and the higher the rank, the older the average age. A 1999 Labour Research survey revealed that of judges appointed or promoted since Labour came to power, 79 per cent went to public school and 73 per cent went to Oxbridge. All but seven of the 692 were white males. It is some-times argued that this produces a reactionary and out-of-touch judiciary and thus impinges on judicial independence. For example, some would argue that judges are likely to be more sympathetic with parties appearing before them with whose social background they can identify.

Training

Compared with their European counterparts, who receive lengthy training for their judicial careers, English judges receive very little, or none. The Judicial Studies Board supervises some brief training for recorders. The Royal Commission on Criminal Justice, 1993, recommended that substantially more resources needed to be devoted to judicial training at this level. Civil train-ing is similarly provided for appointees to the county court.

New High Court judges, however, receive no special training other than the refresher seminars attended by recorders and cir-cuit judges and it is often the case that, at both levels, the appointee's experience as an advocate may be in an entirely dif-ferent area of law from that applied in his judicial role.

The traditional objection to judicial training is that it could undermine judicial independence (*Report of the Working Party on Judicial Studies & Information* 1978). In 1993, the Lord Chancellor announced a programme of ethnic minority awareness training, in response to Hood's research demonstrating racism in senten-cing. All civil judges were given special training in preparation for the new civil procedure rules in 1998 and by 2000 all judges and magistrates were trained in human rights.

Removal

It is a corollary of judicial independence and immunity that judges, especially superior ones, have an entrenched security of tenure, first established in the Act of Settlement 1700. Now, under the Supreme Court Act 1981, every Supreme Court judge "shall hold office during good behaviour, subject to a power of removal by Her Majesty, on an address presented to her by both Houses of Parliament" and the only time this procedure has been used since 1700 was in the case of an Irish Admiralty judge in 1830, for embezzlement. Misbehaviour apparently did not include convictions for drink-driving but, in 1994, Lord Mackay announced that, henceforth, it would. Nevertheless, in 2000 Lord Chancellor Irvine allowed a circuit judge to keep his job despite such a conviction.

The Lord Chancellor may remove an infirm judge, incapacitated from resigning, under the Supreme Court Act 1981, s.11. Under the Courts Act 1971, s.17, he may remove a circuit judge on the grounds of incapacity or misbehaviour, or failure to comply with his conditions of appointment. Judge Bruce Campbell was so removed in 1983 after his well-publicised convictions for smuggling large quantities of whisky and cigarettes.

Complaints

There are no formal powers of reprimand, short of removal. Those aggrieved tend to write to the Lord Chancellor. There are very few famous cases of judges receiving reprimands from the Lord Chancellor, usually for abusing their immunity from defamation actions for offensive things said in court (*e.g.* in 1982 when a judge called a hitch-hiking rape victim "contributorily negligent") or for extra-judicial indiscretion, *e.g.* in 1990, when Judge James Pickles incurred the wrath of Lord Mackay L.C., by calling the Lord Chief Justice "a dinosaur" in a press conference held in a pub. Judges can occasion official displeasure by using the media to broadcast their opinions (*e.g.* Lord Denning during the 1970s and 1980s) but Lord Mackay L.C. announced a policy of encouraging judges to be more publicly outspoken. In 1992, JUSTICE suggested that their proposed Judicial Commission should review judicial conduct and consider complaints and, in 1993, the Royal Commission on Criminal Justice suggested a performance appraisal system for judges which the Labour Government has promised to introduce.

MAGISTRATES

Distinguish between *lay justices* (Justices of the Peace) who are not usually legally qualified and who sit in twos and threes, on average one day per fortnight, and *district judges* (*magistrates' courts*), formally known as *stipendiary magistrates* who are professionally qualified and normally sit alone, full-time. Both types are called magistrates. Their jurisdiction is identical but, through an accident of history, the bulk of the case load in Inner London is heard by district judges while in Outer London and the provinces it is heard by lay justices.

Lay Justices

On January 1, 2000 there were 30,308 lay justices, around half of whom were men. About 2,000 new justices are appointed annually. Most have no legal qualification and all must sit at least 26 half days per year.

Appointment and selection. They are appointed in the name of the Queen to the Commission of the Peace by the Lord Chancellor or, in the Merseyside area, by the Chancellor of the Duchy of Lancaster. They are selected by 95 Advisory Committees, some of which have sub-committees. The committees consist almost exclusively of magistrates and are normally chaired by the Lord Lieutenant of the county, or, in London, by circuit judges. The Lord Chancellor lists several groups who should not be appointed, *e.g.* police and spouses, traffic wardens, probation officers, members of the armed forces, and persons whose work would be incompatible with a magistrate's duties. Appointments of those under 30 are extremely rare.

The Lord Chancellor ran the first national recruitment campaign for magistrates in 1999. Any adult under 65 can apply. Otherwise the many Advisory Committees circulate local political parties and other "established" organisations, inviting them to make recommendations.

Politics and Social Background. Whereas the doctrine of judicial independence ensures that the superior judiciary are above party politics, it has proved impossible to keep it out of the lay magistracy. Many magistrates are local councillors. Indeed, Lord Chancellors have directed Advisory Committees to strive to appoint politically balanced Benches but statistics presented to the House of Commons Home Affairs Committee in 1995 showed magistrates to over-represent Conservatives. The Lord Chancellor is currently seeking an alternative to political balance but consultations showed a geodemographic system to be unpopular.

By its very nature, the work pattern of the lay magistrate excludes certain groups of the population and favours others. Some cannot spare the time to sit, *e.g.* those who travel extensively for their work, those who are establishing businesses and those whose promotion chances depend on their visible efforts at work. These groups tend to be under-represented on the Bench. For some, sitting as a magistrate would cause a financial loss (*e.g.* independent business persons and those who are paid by the hour). J.P.s' loss of earnings allowances are only sufficient to compensate the average to low paid. Groups who can spare the time to sit are over-represented on the Bench (*e.g.* retired persons, teachers and lecturers, top management, housewives with adult children). The over-representation of some of these groups can be exacerbated by the fact that, being readily available, they may sit more often than other magistrates. The Lord Chancellor set a maximum of 100 sittings per year.

The class imbalance of the Bench is a source of continuing concern. The Royal Commission on Justices of the Peace (1948) expressed concern that its statistical survey showed the professions and top management were significantly over-represented on the Bench, with a very low proportion of the waged and research by Hood (1972) and Baldwin (1976) showed that, by then, the imbalance had worsened and had not improved by 1990 (Henham).

Complaints have been made that there are too few members of ethnic minorities on the Bench. The Lord Chancellor, in 1987, acknowledged that the percentage of ethnic minority magistrates on the Bench did not reflect the community as a whole but, despite his recruitment efforts, statistics presented to the House of Commons Home Affairs Committee in 1995 showed that too few minority magistrates are being appointed. Since then, committees have succeeded in recruiting more minority candidates. Lay justices now include 4.5 per cent non-whites.

Training. The Lord Chancellor is empowered to prescribe minimum training requirements for lay justices and their training requirement has been significantly strengthened for the 1990s. It is now as follows:

1. Induction course (before sitting). Three hours' instruction at Bench level, including the trial system and human awareness;

six hours' observation in court, including at an outside Bench;

six hours' participatory decision-making exercises;

a one-hour appraisal session by the clerk.

2. Basic training (year one). Twelve hours' training plus visits to a prison and a young offender institution and an introduction to the probation service.

3. Basic training (years one and two). Eight hours' training, possibly arranged as a residential course.

4. Further training (after three years and each three years thereafter). This should include an element of chairmanship training.

5. Special training. For justices appointed to youth court or family panels. (Service in those courts is restricted to such specially trained panels.) In 1997, Lord Irvine announced that, from September 1998, magistrates training would be altered to emphasise learning by sitting in court and to require magistrates to demonstrate they have acquired knowledge and skills.

A system of mentoring new magistrates was developed in the late 1990s and at the time of writing, 2000, the Judicial Studies Board are discussing the development of a system of performance appraisal based on national standards of competence.

Removal and disqualification. The Lord Chancellor has power, under the Justices of the Peace Act 1997, to remove a magistrate. Most are removed because they fail to fulfil the required 26 sittings per year or because they have moved out of the locality. Justices have been removed for being convicted, for being made bankrupt, for refusing to apply laws they disapproved of and for personal indiscretions.

Additionally, the Lord Chancellor may transfer to the Supplemental List any justice of whom, through age, infirmity or other like cause "it is expedient that he should cease to exercise judicial functions as a justice for that area" or if the justice "declines or neglects to take a proper part in the exercise of those functions" (Justices of the Peace Act 1997, s.8(4)).

Justices are, otherwise, automatically retired on to the Supplemental List at 70 years old. Once on this list, their functions are strictly limited to the non-judicial, for example the authentication of signatures, etc.

District Judges (Magistrates' Courts)

Professional magistrates have exactly the same jurisdiction and powers as lay justices. They are lawyers with a seven-year "general qualification" (as defined by the C.L.S.A., s.71), at the time of appointment, which is made on the recommendation of the Lord Chancellor. In 2000, there were 47 in Inner London and 49 in the provinces. They are supported by 136 deputies. The retiring age is 70, extendable to 72.

The Access to Justice Act 1999 created a unified Bench of district judges, with jurisdiction throughout England and Wales, replacing stipendiary and metropolitan stipendiary magistrates.

Should the Lay Magistracy be Replaced, Nationwide, by Stipendiaries?

The advantages of lay justices are these:
1. Lay involvement in the judicial system (trial by one's peers).
2. They are *very* cheap, compared with professionals, being paid expenses only, which many do not claim. Thousands of experienced lawyers would be needed to supply a nationwide professional magistracy.
3. There is a value, of impartiality, in two or three people taking a decision. It is said that professionals become "case hardened," *i.e.* through over-familiarity with certain offences, their sentencing becoming harsher.

Conversely, it is said district judges have these advantages: 1. They work through the case list more quickly.
2. They are better equipped to deal with the increasingly complex and technical range of criminal offences and sentences available.
3. A professional magistracy would bring us into line with the rest of the Western world.

One alternative would be two lay justices and a professional chairman but this might carry the danger that, as human nature would dictate, the lay magistrates would defer to the professional.

At the time of writing, 2000, the Lord Chancellor has commissioned research into the cost of effectiveness of lay magistrates and district judges but has repeatedly denied he plans to replace the former with the latter. In October 2000, Auld L. J. announced his Review's support of lay justices but noted the widespread support for introduction of a mixed bench.

Magistrates' Clerks

The chief administrator of a Bench or a group of Benches is the justices' chief executive. Both lay justices and professional magistrates are advised by magistrates' clerks. The chief clerk at each court is called the justices' clerk. A justices' clerk may be in charge of more than one Bench and the nationwide trend of the last two decades has been to amalgamate Benches under one clerkship. In 2000, there were 200 justices' clerks, all professionally qualified. The clerks' staff are, like the justices' clerks, appointed and paid by the magistrates' courts committees.

Of course, since many justices' clerks are in charge of more than one court and since most courts have more than one courtroom in session at a time, the justices' clerk necessarily delegates both administrative and advisory functions to his assistants. The staff whose job includes advising magistrates in court are called court clerks or legal advisers, of whom there are over 1,500, and they need not be professionally qualified yet. Delegated legislation requires that, if not professionally qualified, court clerks should be law graduates or equivalent, or possess a special clerks' diploma in magisterial law, or be qualified by five years' experience before 1980. A 1995 survey of court clerks' qualifications showed that only under half were professionally qualified. The Conservative Minister pronounced, in 1996, that he would not effect a policy of requiring all court clerks to be professionally qualified, contrary to the aims of the Justices' Clerks' Society.

This led to the curious situation where, in many provincial courtrooms, the court clerk advising the lay justices is not professionally qualified. More anomalous is the fact that in Inner London, where most cases are heard by district judges, most clerks are professionally qualified.

In 1999, the Labour minister responded to these criticisms and introduced delegated legislation requiring all clerks to be lawyers by 2010 but the over 40s are exempted.

TRIBUNAL MEMBERS

Chairmen of tribunals are most commonly members of the legal profession, sitting as part-timers. Lawyer-chairmen were favoured by the Franks Committee in 1957 and the reasons are obvious: legal expertise to regulate procedure and evidence and to interpret the applicable substantive law. The other two who normally sit with the chairman are seldom legally qualified but are selected, instead, to import an element of expertise into the adjudication. For example, the employment tribunals' members are usually drawn from employers' and employees' organisations; those tribunals concerned with the collection of revenue often appoint accountants and ex-tax inspectors. The Government has been criticised for abolishing lay involvement in some tribunals, in the late 1990s, notably social security tribunals.

Tribunal chairmen are appointed by the Lord Chancellor or selected by the relevant government department or tribunal President from a panel appointed by the Lord Chancellor. Other tribunal members are appointed by the relevant government department, by the Crown or the Lord Chancellor. In many instances, appointments are for three years, renewable, and members are removable by the relevant Minister, with the Lord Chancellor's consent.

The big tribunals, such as the Lands Tribunal or the Employment Appeal Tribunal, need full-time appointees and these are usually of similar status and salary to puisne judges.

THE JURY

Most of what is said in this section relates to trial by jury in the Crown Court, where most juries sit. Juries are also used in coroners' courts and in the civil courts but their use is rare in the latter (see below).

Eligibility

Historically, the jury were the equivalent of today's witnesses, local people who knew something of the defendant or the alleged incident. From the nineteenth century, jury service was confined to owners of property over a certain value. Eventually, all householders became eligible and now the property qualification has been abolished and jury selection is laid down in the Juries Act 1974, as amended by the Criminal Justice Act 1988 and the Criminal Justice and Public Order Act 1994. Those eligible are people on the electoral register, aged 18–70, who have lived in the United Kingdom for five years. Nowhere in the Act does it specify that selection should be random. Indeed Schedule I significantly qualifies randomness by listing those who are ineligible, disqualified or excusable.

Ineligible. The judiciary, legal profession, others concerned with the administration of justice, the mentally ill, the clergy.

Disqualified (as amended by the Juries Disqualification Act 1984).

Those who have ever been sentenced to custody for five or more years and those who, in the last 10 years, have received any prison, borstal, youth custody or suspended sentence or community service order, or who have been placed on probation in the last five years. Those on bail are also disqualified (C.J.P.O. Act 1994).

Excusable as of right. M.P.s and peers, members of the armed forces, medical and similar professions. The Criminal Justice Act 1988 added those over 65 and the C.J.P.O. Act 1994 added members of religious bodies with beliefs or tenets incompatible with jury service.

Discretionary excusal. Section 9(2) of the 1974 Act permits further inroads into randomness by allowing the jury summoning officers to accept excuses from other individuals for good reasons. What is acceptable is, of course, highly subjective. Thus, for example, Baldwin and McConville found in their research published in *Jury Trials* (1979) that, in Birmingham, excuses were readily accepted from mothers of small children, distorting the gender balance. The Criminal Justice Act 1988 gave summoning officers an additional power of discretionary deferral which should lessen the distorting effects of excusal on the overall pattern of jury selection. In 1988, the Lord Chief Justice issued a Practice Direction guiding courts in excusing jurors. Reasons include personal involvement in a case and personal hardship. Additionally, judges may discharge those who are incapacitated through physical disability (C.J.P.O. Act 1994). In 2000, the Court Service introduced a nationwide summoning and excusal system, in an endeavour to ensure consistency.

Selection

Selection from the electoral register is done randomly. At this stage, there are several factors destroying randomness. Most obviously, the electoral register is not accurately representative of the population because of population mobility, house moves, death, and, latterly, because of people declining to register, in an attempt to evade council tax. It is up to the summoning officer which electoral registers he uses and thus which area the jurors will come from. In the 1980s, there were complaints from black defendants that jurors were summoned from white areas. Judges have resisted most attempts to artificially construct mixed race juries but in one trial the judge ordered an adjournment and, in another, ordered a jury to be summoned from a different district, in the hope of selecting a mixed jury.

The group summoned to attend at a particular Crown Court location is called "the panel," from which juries are selected for trials over a certain period (usually two weeks) and the prosecution at this stage may exercise a problematic form of scrutiny known as "vetting."

Vetting

The Attorney-General's 1980 guidelines distinguish between (a) vetting carried out by the police and (b) "authorised checks," requiring his personal consent:

(a) Police may make checks against criminal records, following guidelines set down by the Association of Chief Police Officers, to establish that jurors are not disqualified.
(b) "Authorised checks" which are very rare are carried out only with the Attorney-General's permission, following a recommendation by the D.P.P. The D.P.P. decides what part of the information disclosed should be forwarded to the prosecution (**Note**: *not* the defence). Except in terrorism cases, such checks will not now be carried out in politically motivated cases, or those involving criminal gangs and in, for example, Official Secrets trials, vetting will only be permitted where national security is involved and the hearing is likely to be *in camera*.
(c) Additionally, in cases falling under the guidelines, after an "authorised check," the Attorney-General will con-

sider and, in other cases, the Chief Constable may consider, defence requests for information revealed on jurors.

Challenges to the Array

Once the panel has been assembled, all parties have a common law right, preserved by section 12(6) of the Juries Act 1974, to challenge the whole panel, on the grounds that the summoning officer is biased or has acted improperly, *e.g.* this was attempted in *Danvers* (Crown Court, 1982) by a black defendant, on the grounds that the all-white jury did not reflect the ethnic composition of the community.

Challenge by the Prosecution

Whether or not checks have been made on the panel, the prosecution may exclude any of them from a particular jury by asking them to "stand by for the Crown" without reasons, until the whole panel, except for the last 12, is exhausted. Reasons, "cause," must be given for any further challenges but, with panels often consisting of 100 or more, the prosecution rarely needs to explain its challenges.

The Attorney-General announced, in 1988, that the prosecution's right to stand a juror by without giving reasons would now be limited to two instances:

(i) to remove a "manifestly unsuitable" juror;
(ii) to remove a juror in a terrorist or security trial where the Attorney-General has authorised vetting.

This goes some way towards responding to complaints over the imbalance between prosecution and defence rights of challenge.

Challenges by the Defence

Once the jury are assembled in court, the defence may challenge any number of potential jurors *for cause* (*i.e.* good reason acceptable to the judge) but what is an acceptable "cause" has been qualified by a 1973 Practice Note issued by the Lord Chief Justice, who stated it was contrary to established practice for jurors to be excused on grounds such as race, religion, political beliefs or occupation.

Until recently, the defence could make a certain number of

peremptory challenges, that is, challenges without reasons. This has now been abolished, amidst great controversy, by the Criminal Justice Act 1988. This resulted from unsupported but widespread public allegations that the right to peremptory challenge was being abused by defence lawyers, deliberately trying to skew the jury and the recommendation of the Roskill Committee on fraud trials (1986) that it be abolished. This leaves a gross imbalance between prosecution and defence rights of challenge, which the Criminal Bar Association argued was a breach of Article 6 of the European Convention on Human Rights.

Excusal by the Judge

Under the Juries Act, s.10, the judge may discharge from service any juror about whom there is doubt as to "his capacity to act effectively as a juror" because of physical disability or insufficient understanding of English. Additionally, judges have a common law discretion to discharge jurors and they occasionally interpret this quite broadly.

Controversies Surrounding the Jury

There is an ongoing debate between civil libertarians and others about the pros and cons of retaining the jury and jury equity.

Should the jury be retained and does it inject layman's "equity" into the legal system?

PRO (a) The jury rouses strong emotions and seems to be defended by some historians, civil libertarians, politicians, judges and laypeople as the last bastion of civil liberties. For example, Lord Devlin hailed it as a guardian of democracy: "the lamp that shows that freedom lives" and Blackstone called the jury "the glory of English law . . . the liberties of England cannot but subsist so long as this palladium remains sacred and inviolate" (*Commentaries*, 1768).

It is argued that the jury acts as a check on officialdom, on the judge's power, and a protector against unjust or oppressive prosecution, injecting jury "equity" by deciding guilt or innocence according to a feeling of justice rather than by applying known law to facts proven beyond reasonable doubt.

(b) Additionally, jury supporters argue that a decision by 12 lay people is fairer than one by a judge alone, since it is likely that 12 people will cancel out one another's prejudices.

CON (a) The importance of the jury system is overrated, for example, when given the choice, being charged with a criminal offence "triable either way," the vast majority of defendants choose to appear before magistrates (source: *Annual Criminal Statistics*) and, of the remainder, who opt for the Crown Court, about three-quarters plead guilty and thus are not tried by jury but just sentenced by the judge. Thanks to this and the downgrading of offences as summary, under one per cent of defendants are now tried by jury (Source: *Criminal Statistics*).

(b) The rate of use of civil juries has declined massively since the nineteenth century. The Administration of Justice (Miscellaneous Provisions) Act 1933 imposed limits on the use of civil jury trial, which remains a right only in cases of libel, slander, malicious prosecution, false imprisonment and fraud but, under the Supreme Court Act 1981, the court can refuse jury trial.

(c) By now, civil juries are rarely used (under 400 trials per year) and examining the reasons why people do not opt for them gives an idea of the drawbacks of jury trial:

The Faulks Committee (1974) recommended that juries should no longer be available as of right in defamation actions because, *inter alia*:

(i) Judges were not as remote from real life as popularly supposed.
(ii) Judges gave reasons, whereas juries did not.
(iii) Juries found complex cases difficult.
(iv) Juries were unpredictable.
(v) Juries were expensive (jury trial is more time consuming, as explanations have to be geared for them, not a judge).

Additional reasons given by the anti-jury lobby for the unpopularity of civil juries are:

(vi) They seldom take notes, are not encouraged to do so, and may not be able to remember all the evidence, thus they are likely to be swayed in the jury room by the more dominant characters' interpretation or recollection of events and to be more vulnerable to persuasive rhetoric than a judge.

Their difficulty in understanding evidence is most acute in fraud trials and was considered by the Roskill Committee on Fraud Trials in 1986. Fraud trials are notoriously long (often over 100 days), expensive and highly complicated.

The Committee recommended the jury be abolished in complex criminal fraud cases and be replaced by a Fraud Trials Tribunal of a judge and two lay members with, where appropriate, a knowledge of accountancy and bookkeeping. Calls for the jury's replacement in serious fraud trials have been renewed since the costly Maxwell brothers' trial in 1995–1996 and, in 2000, The Fraud Advisory Panel suggested a number of reforms.

(d) The notion that the jury applies its own equity has no substance. Baldwin & McConville in *Jury Trials* (1979) found no evidence that juries acquitted people in the face of unjust prosecution. On the contrary, perverse verdicts occurred at random. The jury thus had the disadvantage of being unpredictable.

At the time of writing, it appears that Auld L. J.'s Criminal Courts Review will recommend a major restructuring of jury trials.

---

4. THE ADVERSARIAL PROCESS

CIVIL LITIGATION FROM 1999

The Civil Procedure Rules 1998 and over 40 practice directions replaced two separate sets of rules for the High Court and county court, in April 1999. They embodied a radically different approach to civil procedure from what had gone before and were modelled on recommendations by Lord Woolf in *Access to Justice* 1996, better known as the Woolf Report. The background to this "new scenario" is explained below, after the description of the new procedure.

Civil Procedure Act 1997

Section 1 provided for one set of practice rules for the Court of Appeal, High Court and county courts. Section 1(3) "with a view to securing that the civil justice system is accessible, fair and efficient". Section 2 provided a Civil Court Rule Committee to include people "with experience in and knowledge of" consumer affairs and lay advice.

Section 6 established a Civil Justice Council: comprising the Master of the Rolls (which in 1999 was Lord Woolf, who is now the Lord Chief Justice), judges, lawyers, consumer/lay advice and litigant representatives, to keep the civil justice system under review (including A.D.R. and tribunals), advise the Lord Chancellor and suggest research.

Lord Woolf said in the debate on the Bill:

> "When I set out on the inquiry which resulted in my report, I was very conscious that since 1885 there had already been over 60 reports, each urging reform of the civil justice system, yet the situation on which I had to report was one which many commentators described as being in crisis. Why should this be so? It is not because of any callous disregard of their responsibilities by those in charge of the system. It is my belief part of the cause is the absence of a broadly based body which has the clear responsibility for monitoring the justice system as a whole and identifying the areas which are in need of reform".

The 1998 Rules and the New Regime

The overriding objective is set out in Rule 1.1:
  The rules enable the court to deal with a case justly—

  a. ensuring the parties are on an equal footing
  b. saving expense
  c. dealing with the cease in a way which is proportionate
     - to the amount of money involved
     - to the importance of the case
     - to the complexity of the issues
     - to the financial position of parties.
  d. ensuring that it is dealt with expeditiously and fairly and
  e. allotting to it an appropriate share of the court's resources.

The court MUST apply the objective in

  - interpreting the rules
  - exercising their powers.

Pre-action protocols have been issued in personal injury litigation and clinical disputes. These are statements of best practice in negotiation, encouraging exchange of information and putting the parties into a position to settle fairly. Apparently, at the time of writing, 2000, 20 new protocols are being drafted.

Starting proceedings The claimant (formerly plaintiff) or court issues and serves the claim on the defendant. This must include particulars of the claim (statement of case) or they must be served within four months. They may include points of law, witness lists and documents and must include statements of truth and value and specify the remedy sought.

The defendant must, within 14 days:

- admit the claim or
- file a defence (statement of case) or
- acknowledge.

If not, the claimant may request a *default judgment* (Part 12). This means, asking the court to grant his claim as the defendant has not entered a defence. Most cases will end at this point. The defendant may issue a claim against a co-defendant or third party or make a counterclaim (Part 20). The claimant may reply and defend. The parties may write direct to others requesting further information (formerly known as "further and better particulars").

Interim orders The parties may apply for the interim orders listed below. This should be less necessary than before 1999, because of case management—the court may now act on its own initiative. There is an obligation to apply early. Hearings may be by telephone:

- pre-action remedies if urgent
- applications without notice (formerly called *ex parte*)
- extensions or shortening of time
- requiring attendance
- separating or consolidating issues or excluding issues
- deciding the order of issues
- staying (pausing) all or part of the case, hoping for settlement
- interim injunctions/declarations
- freezing injunctions (formerly called *Mareva* injunctions) and search orders (formerly *Anton Piller* orders) may only be ordered by a H.C. judge or authorised judge

- pre-action disclosure (formerly discovery) or inspection, including against non-parties
- interim payments and payments into court

Summary judgment may be initiated by the claimant, defendant or court, where the claim or defence "has no real prospect of success". The court may enter judgment, dismiss the case, strike out a claim, or make a conditional order.

The court's duty to manage cases had already been introduced from 1994 in practice directions, including timetabling, the requirement for skeleton arguments, limitation of oral argument. The duty now includes:

- encouraging parties to co-operate
- identifying issues at an early stage
- deciding promptly which issues can be disposed of summarily
- deciding the order of issues
- encouraging A.D.R.
- helping parties settle
- fixing timetables
- considering cost benefit
- grouping issues
- dealing with a case in the absence of one or more parties
- making use of I.T.
- directing the trial process quickly and efficiently.

Sanctions for failure to comply with case management include striking out, costs and debarring part of a case or evidence. Trials will only be postponed as a last resort. *Procedural judges* manage cases: masters in the Royal Courts of Justice and district judges in the county court and High Court district registries. The court has a great deal of control over what evidence it is prepared to hear and the format in which it is prepared to hear witnesses. Lord Woolf was of the strong opinion that over use of *expert witnesses* by both sides had made litigation costly and unduly adversarial. The assumption is now that one witness will do or, if more than one is permitted, that they will agree a statement pre-trial. Under Part 35, the expert's duty is to help the court and no party may call an expert or use a report without the court's permission. In fast track trials where counsel is briefed, the court cannot normally order costs for a solicitor to accompany her.

Allocation Defended claims are allocated to one of three tracks, once the defendant has completed the allocation questionnaire. The judge may transfer a case to another court.

Small claims: for most actions under £5,000, except:

- personal injuries over £1,000
- disrepair over £1,000
- landlord harassment or unlawful eviction
- allegations of dishonesty

Claims over £5,000 may be allocated to the small claims procedure, by consent.

Fast track for most cases £5–15,000, which can be tried in a day. Oral expert evidence is limited to two fields and one expert per field.

Multi-track claims over £15,000 or over one day's trial.

Claims with no monetary value are allocated where the judge considers they will be dealt with most justly.

Discretionary factors The procedural judge must have regard to:

- the nature of the remedy sought
- the complexity of facts, law and evidence
- the number of parties
- the value of the counterclaim
- oral evidence
- the importance of the claim to non-parties
- the parties' views
- the circumstances of the parties

The Woolf Report suggested the following cases for the multi-track:

- those of public importance
- test cases

- medical negligence cases (now "clinical disputes")
- cases with the right to jury trial

Multi-track cases will normally be transferred out to trial centres but some must stay in the Royal Courts of Justice, *e.g.*:

- specialist cases
- defamation
- fraud
- contentious probate
- claims against the police

District judges have unlimited jurisdiction to assess damages, unless otherwise directed.

Small claims procedure Hearings are meant to be in public (European Convention on Human Rights) but will normally be held in the district judges' chambers, as before 1999. The district judge may adopt any procedure she considers fair, including hearing lay representatives. (Baldwin's research indicated differences). Appeal lies to a circuit judge on law or serious irregularity. Costs are fixed and include the claim fee, £50 per witness and £200 per expert.

Fast track procedure The intention is for the court to maintain "proportionality", which means limiting the costs recoverable from the unsuccessful party. The aim is to increase access to justice by removing uncertainty. The fast track aims to help the parties to obtain justice speedily. The court directs the timetable and fixes the trial date no more than 30 weeks ahead. The intention is to provide little scope for either party to create extra work to gain a tactical advantage. Lord Woolf said it was important for the court to protect the weaker party against oppressive or unreasonable behaviour by a powerful party. Standard directions now include disclosure, the exchange of witness statements, expert evidence, and fixing the trial date. Parties are encouraged to use a single expert, or a court appointed expert. The standard timetable is nine months from the issue of proceedings to trial. An indexed, paginated bundle must be produced to the court three to seven days pre-trial and may include an agreed case summary. The judge pre-reads the bundle. Judges may have Fridays off for pre-reading. Trial costs are fixed according to the amount recovered. Other costs are assessed summarily by the judge after the trial.

Multi-track procedure varies. Simple cases are treated like fast track ones. Complex ones may have several directions hearings:

- a case management conference attended by lawyers familiar with the case, which may require a 500 word case summary
- a pre-trial review of the statement of issues
- other directions hearings.

Disclosure (formerly known as discovery). Lord Woolf thought one of two major generators of unnecessary cost was uncontrolled discovery. Now standard disclosure requires only documents on which a party relies and documents which:

- adversely affect his case
- adversely affect another party's case
- support another party's case
- documents required by a practice direction

The court's power to control evidence The court has power to control the delivery of evidence and whether it is prepared to hear oral, hearsay, or written evidence, etc.

Offers to settle (Part 36) This procedure encourages the parties to settle by financial incentive. It replaces pre-1999 payments into court and *Calderbank* letters. Under the old rules the defendant could make a payment into court and force the plaintiff to take a gamble: take the money or proceed to trial and risk paying both sides costs since the time of the payment in. The intention of the new rules is that allowing the claimant to make an offer to settle alters the balance of power. It includes pre-action formal offers, the claimant's or defendant's offer to settle and the defendant's part 36 payments into court.

Wasted costs the court may make a wasted costs order against a representative if she has acted improperly, unreasonably or negligently and her conduct has caused unnecessary costs to the other party.

A group litigation order may be made to allow for case management in multi-party actions.

General points The reforms are intended to cut the length of trial but may increase the number of trials, as going to trial should become simpler and less expensive. Suitable cases may be disposed without a hearing (Rule 1.4(2)). The statutory right to jury trial is unaffected in deceit, libel, slander, malicious prosecution and false imprisonment cases. Generally, hearings must be in open court. Practice Direction 39 refers to the European Convention on Human Rights. There are exceptions where hearings may be in private (formerly known as *in camera* in chambers), *e.g.*:

- if the hearing involves a child
- mortgage possession cases.

Witness statements count as evidence-in-chief. Supplementary questions may be asked only for "good reason". Money judgments must be complied with within 14 days.

Family procedure is the subject of a special set of rules, not covered by this book. The CPR do not apply to most family proceedings but there are certain exceptions. For instance the cost rules do apply. It is sometimes said that elements of the CPR were copied from existing family procedure. Family judges were well aware already of the need to keep costs and delay down and experts were only used with the court's permission.

The Woolf Reforms and A.D.R. Encouraging and facilitating A.D.R. forms part of case management. Research has produced mixed results and some A.D.R. schemes have not had a high take-up rate, such as the Central London county court's mediation scheme and mediation under the Family Law Act 1996. Anxious to maximize the use of A.D.R., the Lord Chancellor produced a consultation paper on it in 2000. The responses and the paper appear on the L.C.D. website, *www.open.gov.uk/lcd*. Incidentally, an annexe to the paper gives a useful summary of all the different types of A.D.R., fuller than can be provided in this book.

Background to the "Woolf Reforms" of 1999

English civil procedure had been, historically, intensely adversarial and was often referred to in terms of a battle or game. The judge's role was that of a non-interfering umpire. The parties were left to prepare their case, unaided by the court or the other side. Until the 1980s, they kept most of their "cards close to the chest" and it was difficult to assess the strength of the opposition's case. This led to a number of problems, which were described in the literature of Dickens and identified and discussed in over 60 reports in the twentieth century, prior to Lord Woolf's report. Some of the major problems identified were:

Delay, often caused by one or both parties manipulating the pre-trial stages for their own ends. For instance, if the defendant was likely to be ordered to pay substantial damages, it was in his interests to delay proceedings for as many years as possible. The timetabling of civil High Court cases was measured in terms of years, not months. When the case came to court, the length of trial was dictated by the behaviour of the parties and the length of the case they chose to present, with the court out of control.

Inequality of the parties. A battle is only fair if the parties are of equal strength. Inevitably, in most cases, one party would be more powerful, in terms of money, other resources, or information. This is obvious where a consumer was suing a large corporation, or where someone who had suffered negligent surgery was suing an Area Health Authority. This inequality allowed the powerful party to dominate the other into submission and, since the vast bulk of civil cases settled out of court, the suspicion was they often settled on terms more acceptable to the powerful party.

Cost The cost of litigating in the High Court in England and Wales was legendary and measured in terms of hundreds of thousands of pounds.

Reforms Since the 1980s

The Civil Justice Review produced its final report in 1998. Its suggestions were quite radical and attempted to eliminate some of the secretive elements of the pre-trial stage. After its interim report was published, in 1986, the courts issued practice directions to require the exchange of witness statements and make discovery (now disclosure) automatic. It even contemplated whether two tiers of civil court were really necessary. Its most radical achievement was to suggest the enactment of the Courts and Legal Services Act 1990, which gave the county court the same jurisdiction as the High Court, except for certain procedures such as judicial review. The Act enabled the Lord Chancellor to make rules redistributing civil business, shifting most of it down to the county court, where fees were cheaper and procedure simpler.

Hardly had the Act come into force, when a committee of the two sides of the legal profession produced another report, *Civil Justice on Trial—The Case for Change* (1993), otherwise known as the Heilbron Report. It recommended the exchange of skeleton arguments, pre-trial, case management and timetabling by the judge, the reduction of oral argument and an emphasis on shifting civil litigation out of court and into A.D.R. and all of these were introduced by practice directions, from 1994 onwards so the seeds of the Woolf recommendations had already been sown.

Access to Justice, "The Woolf Report", 1996

Defects identified by Lord Woolf were costs, which often exceeded the claim, inequality between powerful and under-resourced litigants; uncertainty, incomprehensibility, fragmentation, with no one responsible overall for civil justice and over-adversarialism, with parties running the cases and ignoring court rules. He recommended case management, with the courts determining and enforcing realistic timetables and suitable procedures. Defended cases will be allocated to one of three tracks, as described above.

The second stage of his inquiry concentrated on medical negligence, housing cases and multi-party actions, where he felt the system failed most conspicuously to meet the needs of litigants. Lord Woolf was concerned to improve access to justice for small business. He drafted a new set of unified rules for the High Court and county court which ultimately became the draft of the present 1999 rules, described above. His "new landscape" has the following features:

- Litigation will be a last resort, with A.D.R. and settlement promoted.
- Litigation will be less adversarial, with an expectation of openness and cooperation and use of single, court appointed experts where possible.

- Simplified procedure with all proceedings commenced by claim and disclosure restricted.
- All cases timetabled (including trial length) and monitored by the court.
- Litigation will be more affordable, predictable (fixed costs in fast track).
- Parties of limited means (unrepresented) will be able to litigate on a more equal footing, with advice services from the courts (leaflets, videos, help lines and IT). Judicial case management will ensure wealthier parties cannot gain tactical advantage.
- A Head of Civil Justice will have overall responsibility (Sir Richard Scott V.C. was appointed in January 1996).
- Judges and courts will be deployed to meet the needs of litigants, with heavier cases heard at trial centres with specialist judges.
- Judges were to be given case management training and encouraged to specialise in such areas as housing and medical negligence.
- Legal aid reform must take account of his recommendations (*e.g.* by providing aid for A.D.R. and funding for court advice services and by recognising the importance of small firms of solicitors, especially in remote areas).
- All recommendations of the Civil Justice Review on providing advice, information and assistance to litigants should be implemented. This was aided by Lord Mackay's creation of the Court Service Agency, with its emphasis on customer service.

Criticisms

The law journals of 1995–1999 contain too much comment to summarise here but the best known are these:

- Many doubted the capabilities of English judges to effect hands on case management, as they have been required to do the opposite, *i.e.* be non-interfering, during their careers.
- Judicial case management would provoke many appeals, as parties would think they had been unfairly treated.
- (Michael Zander) Lord Woolf commissioned no research on what caused delay but blamed it on lawyers, yet other bodies, such as the Cantley Committee, suggested that

the way lawyers operate the adversarial system is a minor cause of delay. "There is not the slightest prospect that these prescribed time limits will be complied with".

- (Zander) the RAND corporation had reached discourging conclusions in research on the effects of judicial case management in the U.S.A. in 1990–1995. It indicated that judges had difficulty in allocating cases to the right track at an early stage. Judges would vary in aptitude. Increasing their discretion would produce inconsistent decisions. Many new procedures would worsen delay. Case management would generate more work for lawyers and increase cost.
- (Adrian Zuckerman) The fixed costs of £2,500 for fast track cases were too much, once V.A.T., expert fees, interlocutory applications and advocacy fees had been added.
- (Zuckerman) "The cause of excessive cost lies not in the complexity of our procedure, but in the incentives that lawyers have to complicate litigation." These interests would defeat Woolf's attempts to reform. Lawyers paid by the hour had an incentive to complicate cases. Lay clients had no means of judging whether their solicitor's work was necessary (*e.g.* interlocutory applications). (Quoting Lord Mackay's White Paper on legal aid reform) the legal aid system gave highest rewards to lawyers who do more work than was necessary.
- (J.A. Jolowicz) The reforms would effect a significant shift away from the adversary system. There was no reason why this should not be done, as adversarial civil justice grew out of jury trial, which is now almost extinct. If the Woolf proposals resulted in a move towards achieving the aim of substantive, as well as procedural justice, they were to be welcomed.
- Responses to the many objections to the Woolf report were made by District Judge Greenslade at (1997) 147 N.L.J. 1147, 1215, 1252, 1293.

Implementation of Woolf

Many of the recommendations made in Lord Woolf's 1995 interim report had been implemented by 1996 and were listed in his final report. In May 1997, the Conservative Lord Chancellor was replaced by Labour's Lord Irvine. He appointed Peter Middleton to review both the Woolf Report and the reform of legal aid. In October 1997, Lord Irvine responded to Peter Middleton's report, in a speech to the Law Society, setting out the Labour Government's proposals for action in response to the Woolf report:

- Expand small claims jurisdiction to £5,000.
- Leave the small claims limit at £1,000 in personal injury cases.
- Accept Woolf's plans for judicial case management.
- Multi-track and fast track would be implemented by April, 1999 but fast track limit should be £15,000, not £10,000 as Woolf had suggested.
- Costs in the fast track would be fixed.
- The cost of civil courts should be met by people who use them but the civil fee structure was "irrational and hopelessly out of date" so needed reforming. Exemptions from court fees should be extended to more groups on state benefits.

Comments on the Woolf reforms since implementation in 1999

- Nigel Foster, a law lecturer, gave a condemnatory personal account of his experience bringing a small claim under the new rules ((2000) 150 N.L.J. 318). His claim took nine months, involved four court appearances and at least six judges. Evidence rules were applied inconsistently. The trial judge had neither pre-read the papers nor managed the case.
- Richard Harrison ((2000) 150 N.L.J. 541) commented that processing cases brusquely, efficiently and driving litigants away from the system did not mean that they were enjoying "access to justice". Increased cost and frustration was caused by the courts' inflexibility in allowing the parties to manage cases themselves. This would clash with the requirements of the Human Rights Act. Constant amendments to the rules rendered them very complex, the opposite of one of Woolf's major objectives.
- On the other hand, Robert Turner, Senior Master in the High Court, welcomed the new rules ((2000) 150 N.L.J. 49). The pervading adversarial approach had gone and been replaced by a degree of co-operation. Settlements were achieved earlier, procedures were defining the real

issues between the parties and solicitors would find the quicker rate of disposal allowed them to do more work. In the short term, however, the new rules had not succeeded in attacking cost, delay and complexity because the new system was costly at the commencement of the action ("front loaded"); the new procedures with pre-action protocols, allocation and listing questionnaires and case management conferences, etc., were more complex and many county courts were struggling with implementation so delays were occurring.

- A survey of heads of legal departments of U.K. companies by Eversheds, lawyers, found 54 per cent of respondents considered civil litigation improved in 1999–2000. 52 per cent found litigation quicker but only 22 per cent considered it cheaper. 43 per cent were settling cases earlier. Clients no longer sought aggressive, uncompromising lawyers. Disputes were handled differently and 41 per cent had used A.D.R. Only 24 per cent thought litigants were getting better justice. 44 per cent said they were not. 19 per cent said costs had risen.

- Another survey by Wragge & Co. of in-house commercial lawyers found 81 per cent of respondents thought courts did not have enough resources. 89 per cent liked the changes and found litigation quicker, 41 per cent found costs cut and 80 per cent found A.D.R had proved popular. (Both surveys are summarised in *The Times*, May 2, 2000).

- the Civil Justice Council published its first report in September 1999. They were concerned about the high allocation fee (£80) for small claims and about delay in introducing new I.T. into the courts.

PRE-TRIAL CRIMINAL PROCEDURE

In 1990–1991, public faith in the English criminal justice system reached an all time low, with the official acknowledgment of a number of miscarriages of justice which had resulted in many innocent people wasting decades in gaol, only to be freed after years of campaigning by pressure groups and journalists had raised the cases to *causes célèbres* status. The most notable of these cases are those of *The Guildford Four*, *The Maguires*, *The Birmingham Six*, *The Winchester Three* and *The Broadwater Farm Three*.

In 1991, in response to public anxiety over all this, the Home Secretary appointed a Royal Commission on Criminal Justice, which reported in 1993. Its terms of reference were to examine the effectiveness of the Criminal Justice System in securing the conviction of the guilty and the acquittal of the innocent. In this section and the sections on trial and criminal appeals, I incorporate the main recommendations of the R.C.C.J. There is only space here to mention the few most significant recommendations of the R.C.C.J. The Summary of Recommendations is reproduced at (1993) 143 N.L.J. 993 and 1028. These recommendations have been heavily criticised, notably by lawyers, who have drawn attention to the number of recommendations which would ease the task of the prosecution, rather than strengthen protection for the defendant. This surprised commentators, in view of the fact that the Commission was set up in response to some of this century's most famous wrongful convictions. Students will find many critiques of the Commission's report in 1993 legal news journals (*e.g. New Law Journal* and *Legal Action* and, in more depth, in *The Criminal Law Review* for November and December 1993 and a special 1994 issue of the *Journal of Law and Society* entitled *Justice and Efficiency*).

In 1997, the Conservative Home Secretary received a Review of Delay in the Criminal Justice System known as the Narey Report. Many of its recommendations were enacted in the Crime and Disorder Act 1998. In 2000, the Lord Chancellor asked Auld L.J. to conduct yet another review of the criminal process, called the Criminal Courts Review. Students should look out for his 2001 report at *http://www.criminal-courts-review.org.uk*.

Prosecution

The Prosecutors.

The Attorney-General. His consent is required by statute for prosecutions of national interest or sensitivity (*e.g.* certain prosecutions under the Official Secrets Act). He can also enter a *nolle prosequi*, to stop a prosecution (*e.g.* if it is vexatious or he discovers the defendant is dying).

The Director of Public Prosecutions. In addition to heading the Crown Prosecution Service, about 60 statutes require his consent to prosecution, mostly to serious offences, but he is very seldom involved personally in a decision. In 1997, the Law Commission suggested drastic reduction in the number of offences where the A.G.'s or D.P.P.'s consent is required. The House of Lords held, in *Kebilene* (2000) that the D.P.P.'s decision to prosecute is not judicially reviewable in the absence of bad faith or dishonesty.

Public bodies, with statutory prosecution powers (*e.g.* The Post Office, for T.V. licence offences, H.M. Customs and Excise for V.A.T. offences).

Private persons. Private prosecutions were preserved on the recommendation of the Royal Commission on Criminal Procedure (1980).

The Crown Prosecution Service. This was created as a national prosecution service by the Prosecution of Offences Act 1985, on the recommendation of the Royal Commission on Criminal Procedure. Until then, most prosecutions were instituted by the police, from individual constabularies. Critics, including JUSTICE, thought this was anomalous, as most other legal systems used national prosecution services, and undesirable, as the decision to prosecute was not made independently.

The C.P.S. has the discretion to prosecute and stop proceedings. It can ask the police to investigate offences but it cannot order them to do so. It has no investigatory facilities. The R.C.C.J. considered whether the C.P.S. should have the power to supervise police investigations, as in Scotland or European jurisdictions. They decided against it but recommended strengthening police consultation with the C.P.S. in directing and furthering their investigations. They considered the high rates of discontinuance of prosecutions and directed acquittals and recommended that the C.P.S. be more vigilant in ensuring full preparation of cases coming to the Crown Court.

The Narey report (1997) recommended that C.P.S. non-lawyers should be able to prosecute guilty pleas in the magistrate's court and this was enabled by the Crime and Disorder Act 1998. It also recommended putting C.P.S staff into police stations to create a closer working relationship and prompt the speedy preparation of files.

The C.P.S. are guided in their decisions whether to prosecute by their *Code For Crown Prosecutors* (2000). They apply a two stage evidential and public interest test.

Bail

The Bail Act 1976 introduced a statutory right to bail. Magistrates may refuse bail only if they believe the defendant will fail to surrender to custody, or commit an offence or will interfere with witnesses. The court must have regard to the nature and seriousness of the offence and the probable disposal of the defendant, his character and community ties, etc., his previous bail record and the strength of evidence against him. During the late 1980s concern arose over the number of offences committed whilst on bail. The Criminal Justice and Public Order Act 1994 added another exception to the right to bail where the defendant was already on bail at the time of the alleged new offence. Further, it prohibited bail for those charged with murder, rape, manslaughter and attempts where they have previously been convicted of such an offence. Because of the European Convention on Human Rights, this had to be amended by the Crime and Disorder Act 1998 to permit the court to grant bail in exceptional circumstances.

The Bail (Amendment) Act 1993 gives the prosecution a right to appeal to the Crown Court against the grant of bail by magistrates, in relation to certain serious offences. The accused is not entitled to be present at the appeal, if represented, and the Magistrates' Association opposed the Act on this ground.

Mode of Trial—Crown Court or Magistrates' Court?

Indictable cases have to be tried in the Crown Court and summary offences in the magistrates' court but in the category of median seriousness, "triable either way," the magistrates may send a case up to the Crown Court, if they consider it too serious, or the defendant may elect to be dealt with by the Crown Court. The R.C.C.J. inferred, from 1990 research by Moxon and Hederman, that too many Crown Court cases could more appropriately be dealt with in the magistrates' court. This resulted from defendants opting for Crown Court jury trial, then pleading guilty and from magistrates sending up unimportant cases. The R.C.C.J., very controversially, recommended removing the defendant's overriding right to choose jury trial. They reiterated that, while research had shown that the acquittal rate seemed to be higher in the Crown Court, it also showed that, in matched cases, sentencing was harsher and many defendants later regretted their decision to opt for the Crown Court.

Then, in 1995 the Home Office published a consultation paper on *Mode of Trial*. It suggested three options for resolving the problem identified by the R.C.C.J.: classify more offences as summary only, remove the defendant's right to elect or require magistrates to ask defendants to indicate their plea before taking a decision on mode of trial. The Government opted for the last of these, which is now enacted in section 49 of the Criminal Procedure and Investigations Act 1996 and is now known as the "plea before venue" procedure. The intention behind this section is that magistrates will then hear summarily all either way cases where the defendant indicates a guilty plea, unless, of course, the magistrates consider their sentencing powers too low, in which case they retain the option of committing the defendant to the Crown Court. The aim is to shift yet more criminal business down from the Crown Court into the cheaper magistrates' court. Even before the section was brought into force, however, in February 1997, the Conservative Home Secretary introduced a consultation paper, *Review of Delay in the Criminal Justice System* (the Narey Report). This again suggested dispensing with the defendant's trial option and leaving it to the magistrates to decide which court should hear the case. Three months later, the Labour Government replaced the Conservatives.

In 1998, the Labour Home Secretary, Jack Straw, published "Determining Mode of Trial in Either Way Cases—A Consultation Paper" (Home Office website, *www.homeoffice.gov.uk*). In it, he set out the familiar arguments on abolishing the defendant's right to elect jury trial, as follows:

For Action

- The right was not ancient. It only dated from 1855 and had nothing to do with Magna Carta.
- 22,000 defendants elected for Crown Court trial in 1997 but most changed their plea to guilty, after significant inconvenience and worry to victims and witnesses and considerable extra cost.
- By definition, elected cases are those which magistrates have determined are suitable for themselves. The mode of trial decision should be based on objective assessment by the court of the gravity of the case, not the defendant's perception of what is advantageous to him, such as a greater prospect of acquittal.
- It is questionable whether defendants opt for jury trial to

defend their reputation, as nine tenths of those electing already had previous convictions.

- Most defendants elect because they want to delay proceedings, to apply pressure to the Crown to accept a guilty plea to a lesser offence, to deter witnesses or to put off the evil day.
- Few other jurisdictions allow the defendant such an element of choice (*e.g.* Scotland).

Arguments in Favour of the Status Quo

- The right helps to promote confidence in the criminal justice system.
- Whereas magistrates, in applying *The National Mode of Trial Guidelines* are broadly concerned with the seriousness of the offence, it is the defendant's reputation which the public sees as a justification for continuing to allow the election.
- When people who have never been accused of a crime defend the right, it is usually on the basis that they would want such a right if they were charged with something of which they were innocent.
- It is assumed that Crown Court trial is fairer. Defendants mainly elect because they rightly believe they have a higher chance of acquittal.
- Some arguments go to merits of trial by jury, for example, the jury's capacity to acquit contrary to legal proof of guilt.

One proposal in the paper was to take away the right of those defendants who had previous convictions and who had, therefore, already lost their reputations. Consequently, Jack Straw introduced into the House of Commons the Criminal Justice (Mode of Trial) Bill, in 1999. This would have abolished the defendant's right to elect, placing the mode of trial decision in the magistrates' hands. The prosecutor and accused would have had a right to make representations. The bench would have to take into account the nature of the case, whether the circumstances make the offence serious, whether magistrates' sentencing powers would be adequate, whether the accused's livelihood or reputation would be damaged and any other relevant circumstances. The magistrates could take account of the defendant's previous convictions. In small cases of theft, where the sum involved was under £5,000, the magistrates would be obliged to treat it as an offence triable only summarily.

The Bill attracted much criticism, notably from the Bar, the Law Society, the Society of Black Lawyers and from civil rights groups such as the Legal Action Group. L.A.G. argued the following (*Legal Action*, September 1998):

- The main reason defendants opted for jury trial was that they rightly saw their chances of obtaining justice in the Crown Court as significantly higher. In 1997, 62 per cent of defendants who pleaded not guilty to some or all counts were acquitted. Having a professional judge oversee the case was as important as having a jury. 38 per cent were acquitted because the judge discharged the case and a further 16 per cent on the judge's direction.
- Electing jury trial brings into play a range of other safeguards, such as greater disclosure of the prosecution case. (This point was also made by many other commentators.)
- Removing the right to elect would significantly disadvantage black defendants. They more frequently elect for the Crown Court. Research indicates that this results in more of them being acquitted or having the charges against them dropped.
- Removing the right ignores the effect that other procedural changes will have in minimising defendants' manipulation of the system.
- The suggestion that defendants elect jury trial to put off the evil day is not borne out by research.
- Delays would increase, caused by mini-trials on venue.
- In opposition, Jack Straw had called the proposal "shortsighted".

Wolchover and Heaton-Armstrong added ((1998) 148 N.L.J. 1614 and see 150 N.L.J. 158.):

- It is the inherent superiority of jury trial which makes it essential for defendants to elect for it.
- The Labour Party is normally associated with protection of civil liberties.
- A defendant who delays a guilty plea to obtain some advantage cannot expect the same sentence discount as one who pleads earlier and, since 1986, advocates have had a duty to warn defendants of this.

- Tactical elections will continue to decline because of the "plea before venue" procedure and because of section 48 of the Criminal Justice and Public Order Act 1994, which allowed the sentencing court to take account of the timing of the guilty plea.
- As experienced defence counsel, they denied that defendants caused delay to "put off the evil day". On the contrary, the most frequent and obvious cause of a last minute plea was the defendant's loss of courage.
- The argument is about the loss of a traditional commonlaw right.
- Loss of liberty is no less serious for an habitual thief than loss of good name for someone with no previous convictions.

Courtney Griffiths Q.C. (*Counsel*, April 1999) added:

- Research by the Runnymede Trust, 1990, showed that, whereas under one third of white defendants, given the option, elected for jury trial, 45 per cent of black defendants elected.
- This is an intelligent choice. Only two per cent of magistrates are non-white. Home Office research at Leicester magistrates' court showed white defendants had a substantially better chance of being granted bail and were less likely to receive immediate custodial sentences than blacks. (Incidentally, when the research was completed in 1999, it showed the reverse. Magistrates acquitted more Asians and blacks than whites. Lee Bridges, however, produced another research study which indicated the opposite).

A number of other commentators emphasised that jury trial is inherently superior to summary trial, especially as listing for a Crown Court trial triggered a much more careful review of the case by the C.P.S., which would often result in dropping the case or reducing the charges. This also implied that, if magistrates were to decide on mode of trial, they would be doing so on inadequate information. Further, at the Crown Court, a professional judge reviews the strength and admissibility of the evidence, whereas magistrates are both fact-finders and arbiters of the law. Nigel Ley ((1999) 149 N.L.J. 1316) drew attention to the fact that magistrates do not take notes of evidence or give reasons, that defendants in theft cases were often refused legal aid and that solicitors in magistrates' courts were often ignorant of the law, as were magistrates' clerks. Some critics pointed out that magistrates' courts are seen as police courts, or magistrates are seen as part of the Establishment and magistrates are not as socially and ethnically diverse as the jury.

A *New Law Journal* editorial ((1999) 149 N.L.J. 549) argued that there were other ways of cutting down the cost and length of jury trials, such as reducing jurors to six, to have them sit in the magistrates' court and let lay justices do the sentencing, to cut out the opening statement and permit the judge to sum up only on law.

This first Bill was heavily defeated in the House of Lords, in January 2000. The Home Secretary replaced it with the Criminal Justice (Mode of Trial) Number 2 Bill, which was again defeated in the House of Lords in autumn 2000. Discarded is the requirement that justices consider the impact of a conviction on a person's reputation or job before they decide on mode of trial and added is a right of appeal against the magistrates' decision to the Crown Court. This had not satisfied the critics. Michael Zander and Lee Bridges ((2000) 150 N.L.J. 366,855) said that not allowing the court to take account of the defendant's reputation or livelihood was even worse. Some pointed out that the new right of appeal would add to delay. Many think the timing of the Bill is inappropriate, in the middle of Lord Justice Auld's comprehensive review of the criminal courts.

Committal Proceedings

Almost all defendants in the Crown Court used to be committed for trial by magistrates, whose job it was to certify that there was a prima facie case against them. Mostly this was a quasi-administrative paper exercise, whereby the magistrates simply accepted the defence lawyer's assurance that she was satisfied from the prosecution papers that there is a sufficient case against the defendant. The R.C.C.J. decided that committals served no useful purpose and should be replaced by simple transfer proceedings. The Narey Report 1997 recommended that indictable offences be sent direct to the Crown Court. The Conservative government made unsuccessful attempts to replace committal proceedings and they have now been abolished for indictable only offences by section 51 of the Crime and Disorder Act 1998.

The magistrates may send the defendant and co-accused directly to the Crown Court.

Pre-trial Disclosure of Evidence

At common law and in statute, requirements for pre-trial disclosure had become more extensive and complex since the 1980s. From 1981, the Attorney General had required the prosecution to make available to the defence all unused material, with certain exceptions. The picture became more complex after several miscarriages of justice in the 1990s and the courts found it difficult to strike a balance between the defendant's interest in seeing all the material gathered in the investigation and the prosecution's interest in keeping sensitive material (such as the identity of an informant). At the same time, inroads were made into the defendant's right of silence by requiring him to provide information in certain cases. For instance, expert evidence had to be disclosed, since 1987 and those charged with serious fraud could be faced with a list of written questions from the serious fraud office. The R.C.C.J. recommended a statutory scheme of disclosure. They were particularly anxious to stop "ambush defences", where an unpredictable defence is raised at trial. This was effected by sections 34–39 of the C.J.P.O. Act 1994, which qualifies the defendant's right of silence (see below).

The Criminal Procedure and Investigations Act 1996, Part I, enacts a statutory scheme of disclosure which was brought into force in 1997.

Primary disclosure by the prosecutor is required by section 3. He must disclose to the defence any previously undisclosed material which he has inspected, in accordance with a code and which in his opinion might undermine the prosecution case, or give to the accused a written statement that there is no such material. This section has been fiercely criticised by defence lawyers because the prosecutor will determine what he must disclose. Section 4 requires the prosecutor to give to the accused the schedule of non-sensitive material received by the prosecutor in accordance with a code of practice provided for under the Act.

Disclosure by the accused, which has also been subject to forceful criticism, as eroding the presumption of innocence, is introduced by section 5. It requires the accused to give a defence statement to the court and to the prosecutor, if the case it to be heard in the Crown Court and if the prosecutor has fulfilled primary disclosure. It is a written statement, setting out in general terms the nature of the accused's defence, indicating the matters on which he takes issue with the prosecution and giving the particulars of any alibi. Under section 6, the defendant may make a voluntary defence statement, if he is to be tried summarily. Section 7 provides for secondary prosecution disclosure of any previously undisclosed material, after the defence statement. Section 8 allows the accused to apply for disclosure of material by the prosecutor, where he has reasonable cause to believe there is previously undisclosed material which might aid his defence. Section 9 places a continuing duty on the prosecutor.

The prosecutor need not disclose material which has been obtained by interception of communication (which means phone-tapping, etc.) or where the prosecutor concludes it is not in the public interest to do so (such as information from an informant). Section 11 allows the court to comment and to draw "such inferences as appear proper" where the defence disclosure is defective or too late. The Home Secretary is empowered to make regulations about the timing of disclosure.

Sections 14 and 15 allow the defendant to seek a court review of a non-disclosure decision. The court must rule whether non-disclosure is in the public interest. Whether disclosure is in the public interest will still be determined by the old common law rules. Otherwise, the statute replaces common law.

This statutory scheme of disclosure remains problematic, espeically in the context of the Human Rights Act 1998 (see below).

Plea Bargaining

This can mean one of two things:

1. A deal between prosecution and defence, as described above, where the prosecution drop a serious charge in exchange for a guilty plea to a lesser charge (charge bargaining).
2. A change of plea from not guilty to guilty in exchange for a lower sentence.

This first is endemic and well-known in the Crown Court and equally widespread but less publicised in the magistrates' courts.

The second, well-known and widely used in the United States, is illegal and impracticable here because judges cannot take part in it (see *Turner*) and our prosecutors cannot recommend sentences.

The effects of plea bargaining and other pressures on the accused to plead guilty are the topic of much socio-legal research (notably Baldwin and McConville's *Negotiated Justice* (1977) and Bottoms & McClean's *Defendants in The Criminal Process* (1976)) but, sadly, we only have space to examine the legal position: *R. v. Turner* (CA 1970) affirmed by a 1976 Practice Direction, held that:

(a) Counsel can advise the defendant (how to plead) in strong terms provided he makes it clear the defendant has a free choice.

(b) There must be free access between counsel and judge but any discussion with the judge must take place before both counsel.

(c) Generally, the judge should "never indicate the sentence which he is minded to impose" and never indicate he would impose a severer sentence following a "not guilty" plea.

(d) He may not indicate that, having read the papers, he would impose a certain type of sentence, following a guilty plea.

(e) A judge *may* say that, whatever the plea, the sentence will take a particular form.

The R.C.C.J. recommended that the system of rewarding defendants for pleading guilty should be formalised. The earlier the guilty plea, the higher the sentence discount. Judges should be permitted to indicate, in advance of trial, the highest sentence they were prepared to give. The late Lord Chief Justice Taylor spoke out against this recommendation and in favour of *Turner*. Only the first part of the recommendation has been enacted in section 48 of the Criminal Justice and Public Order Act 1994 now the Crime (Sentences) Act 2000. This puts a duty on the court, in sentencing a guilty pleader, to take into account the stage at which he pleaded guilty and to announce in open court any resultant sentence reduction. This, of course, simply formalises the existing system of rewards for early guilty pleas. It does not introduce plea bargaining as the Americans know it but it may affect (c), above. For a critique of plea bargaining, see Darbyshire, *Criminal Law Review*, November 2000.

The Plea and Directions Hearing

A 1995 Practice Direction requires these hearings prior to Crown Court trials. They are very brief, designed to prepare for the trial and fix a trial date. In all class one or serious or complex cases, the prosection provides a summary, identifying issues of law and fact and estimating trial length. The accused is arraigned and his plea entered. Following a not guilty plea, the parties are expected to inform the court of witnesses and any special requirements for trial. If the plea is guilty, the judge should, if possible, proceed to sentence, after hearing a plea in mitigation. Where the judge is considering a custodial sentence or non-custodial alternative, she may require a pre-sentence report or, where appropriate, a psychiatric or medical report.

Pre-trial Hearings

These are not new but have been put onto a statutory footing by Parts III and IV of the Criminal Procedure and Investigations Act 1996. Prior to the swearing in of the jury, the judge may order a preparatory hearing for one of the following purposes: identifying important issues; assisting the jury's comprehension of those issues; expediting proceedings or assisting the judge's trial management. She may hear arguments and rule on points of law and admissibility of evidence. She may require detailed case statements and require the prosecution evidence and any explanatory material to be prepared in a form which she considers is likely to help the jury understand it. Judges have always heard such arguments in the absence of the jury but dealing with these questions pre-trial may prevent interruptions of the trial, where the jury are sent out and kept waiting. They are modelled on preparatory hearings in serious or complex frauds, made under the Criminal Justice Act 1987.

Speeding Up Justice

As mentioned above, the 1997 Narey Report, *Review of Delay in the Criminal Justice System* was written by a lone civil servant but it was remarkably successful, in that many of its recommendations are enacted in the Crime and Disorder Act 1998, as listed below and elsewhere. The magistrates' courts where the reforms were piloted cut the disposal time of all offenders by around two thirds.

- C.P.S. staff in police stations.
- Use of C.P.S. non-lawyer staff to review and present cases (s. 53, C.D.A. 1998).
- Introduction of early first hearings for straightforward guilty pleas in magistrates' courts.
- Introduction of early administrative hearings for contested cases (s. 50).
- Additions to the powers of single justices and justices' clerks to assist case management (s. 49 C.D.A. and the Justices' Clerks' Rules 1999).

The Government also created a Youth Justice Board, Youth Offending Teams and a set of new procedures to speed up and co-ordinate the processing, treatment and rehabilitation of young offenders.

In 1999, the Government produced another consultation paper on speeding up justice in the Crown Court, called *Transforming the Crown Court*. It proposes rigorous case management and case preparation, on the spot fines for lawyers' delays, new technological support for judges and new levels of customer service for witnesses, victims and jurors. A number of judges have been critical of changes proposed in their working patterns.

The Effect of the Human Rights Act 1998 and the European Convention on Human Rights on Criminal Procedure

As explained earlier in the book, the 1998 Act incorporated the Convention rights into English law in 2000. This has had and will have profound effects on many aspects of criminal procedure:

- Defendants will be able to use a Convention breach as a defence or as grounds of appeal.
- Article 8 guarantees the right to private life, allowing interference only where necessary for national security and public safety, or the prevention of crime and disorder. Surveillance methods, such as phone tapping and bugging must be prescribed by law, with a system of accountability.
- Art. 6(3)c grants the right to legal assistance to everyone charged with a criminal offence. A request cannot be

denied. In *Murray v. U.K.* (1996) the European Court of Human Rights considered legal advice crucial to a defendant who exercised his right of silence. (This implies that the English provision, under the C.J.P.O. Act 1994 requires a lawyer's presence in interrogation). In *Condron v. U.K.* (2000), the ECHR held, applying the Art 6 right to a fair trial, it was inappropriate to draw an adverse inference, under the Criminal Justice and Public Order Act 1994, where defendants explained they had maintained silence on their lawyer's advice.

- In *Saunders v. U.K.* (1997) the ECHR held that enforced answers to D.T.I. questions, pre-trial, violated the privilege against self-incrimination.
- The ECHR has held that an accused's right to communicate in confidence with his lawyer is an essential element of Art. 6(3)c, right to a fair trial. This will require adequate facilities to be provided in the police station and courts.
- The Law Commission has considered whether our laws on bail breach the Convention. As discussed above, bail rules have had to be altered but there are outstanding problems on bail, in the light of Article 5, the right to liberty and Article 6(2) presumption of innocence. The courts will need to act on more substantial evidence, keep bail decisions under constant review, keep in mind the presumption of innocence and give full reasons, not just tick-box reasons which are now handed down.
- Art. 6 requires the defence to be given adequate time and facilities for preparation of the defence.
- Art. 6 requires the accused to be granted legal aid where he cannot afford representation, if the interests of justice so require. The criteria applicable under the Access to Justice Act 1999 appear to be compliant.
- Many critics say the statutory regime for disclosure under the Criminal Procedure and Investigations Act 1996 falls foul of Art. 6 in various ways:
  - Obligatory prosecution disclosure is too limited.
  - In magistrates' courts there is no compulsory prosecution disclosure in summary cases.
  - There is concern over the increase in prosecution claims of public interest immunity (P.I.I.), where, for example, they seek to keep an informant's identity secret. The 2000 decision of the ECHR in *Rowe and Davies v. U.K.*

is very important. In the defendants' murder trial, the prosecution had withheld a number of items of evidence on P.I.I. grounds. The ECHR found a fundamental breach of the applicants' right to a fair trial. The prosecutor should disclose all material in their possession, both for and against the accused. The ECHR held, though, that there is no absolute right to disclosure. It may be overridden by national security or the need to protect witnesses. The Government says present P.I.I. procedure now conforms with the Convention. The Attorney General issued guidelines on disclosure in 2000.

- The ECHR has held that the accused is entitled to be present at trial.
- Art. 6(3)c establishes an unqualified right to a free interpreter.
- The ECHR has held that a costs order against an acquitted defendant violates the presumption of innocence, under Art 6(2).
- The burden of proof is on the prosecutor, under Art 6(2). In 1999, the ECHR held that the Prevention of Terrorism (Temporary Provisions) Act 1989 violated the presumption of innocence.
- The child murderers of Jamie Bulger took the U.K. Government to the ECHR, alleging they had been denied a fair trial under Art. 6 (*T. and V. v. UK*, 1999). The Court agreed that the formality and ritual of the Crown Court trial must have been intimidating and incomprehensible to 11 year old children. Consequently, in 2000, the L.C.J. issued a Practice Direction requiring that youth trials should take account of the age, maturity and development of the defendant. Robes and wigs should not normally be worn.
- The convention, not domestic law, determines whether proceedings are civil or criminal so default proceedings for fine and council tax defaulters will almost certainly be classed as criminal. The proceedings arguably breach Art. 6, as the magistrates' clerk acts as legal adviser to the justices as well as representing the Chief Executive, the enforcement officer.
- Many commentators feel magistrates' clerks will be obliged to give all their advice to the justices in open court.

- A problem arises over rulings on the *admissibility of evidence in the magistrates' court.* In law, magistrates must determine admissibility issues and, if they rule evidence inadmissible, then cast it out of their minds in the trial. This is said to violate Art. 6.
- The Convention requires a reasoned decision. Nevertheless, in *Gregory v. U.K.* the ECHR held that the secrecy of jury deliberations did not render a trial unfair. Magistrates' courts are not courts of record, rendering appeals difficult. The Convention will require magistrates to keep notes of trial and give reasoned decisions.
- In *Sander v. U.K.* (2000) the ECHR ruled that the defendant's fraud trial had been in breach of the Art. 6 because one of the jurors had warned the judge that the jury might not be impartial because some of them were making racist jokes.

THE TRIAL PROCESS GENERALLY

Here we examine the characteristics of the trial in the adversarial process. The trial is its focal point but it must be remembered that a trial occurs in only a tiny minority of cases. The vast majority of defendants in the criminal courts plead guilty and so appear only to offer a plea in mitigation and to be sentenced and, in the civil courts, most cases are settled or judgment is entered in default.

It is important to understand that there are significant differences between civil and criminal trials, such as the degree of proof required and evidential differences, such as the rule against hearsay. The adversarial model cannot apply as well to criminal trials as it does to civil because the defendant is faced with such a powerful opponent: the state.

The Concept of Judge as Arbiter

The essence of the role of the English judge, or magistrate, is that he acts as an unbiased umpire whose job it is to listen to evidence presented to him by both sides, without interfering in the trial process. This is often contrasted with the role of European first instance judges who perform an inquisitorial role, themselves directing criminal investigations, cross-examining the defendant and collecting evidence for the trial court. Of course, there is no comparable English equivalent.

The Practical Meaning of Judge as Arbiter

1. Summoning witnesses. The judge and court, do not, generally select witnesses.

2. The conduct of the trial. The judge does not interfere in the presentation of evidence by examining and cross-examining witnesses him or herself. This is left to the parties or their advocates. The role of the judge was set down clearly by Lord Denning M.R. in *Jones v. National Coal Board* (CA 1957) and can be summarised thus: he should:

(a) listen to all the evidence, only interfering to clarify neglected or obscure points;
(b) see that advocates behave and stick to the rules;
(c) exclude irrelevancies and discourage repetition;
(d) make sure he understands the advocates' points;
(e) at the end, make up his mind where the truth lies.

3. The judge's expertise on law and fact. Generally speaking, the judge relies on the advocates to present legal and factual arguments. Of course, the specialist judges of, say, the Admiralty Court and tribunal members are appointed because they need a certain level of understanding to appreciate specialist argument. A judge can, if a vital precedent has been ignored, invite counsel's arguments upon it.

The rule of non-intervention, set out above, does not apply to *legal* argument addressed to the judge. Students watching this in court will see that very often a dialogue goes on between counsel and the judge, especially in civil cases and the appellate courts. Following Lord Woolf's recommendations, civil judges are becoming much more interventionist in all aspects of case management.

English law is emphatic that the judge or magistrates or magistrates' clerk must not interfere in a case. To do so invokes accusation of a breach of natural justice. Justice must be seen to be done.

The rule of non-interference is subject to certain exceptions:

(a) Small Claims in the county court. Research by Appleby (1978) showed some registrars employed an inquisitorial technique. Many of those who appear are unrepresented and, therefore, the progress of the case depends on the district judge being

somewhat interventionist. The Civil Justice Review 1988 recommended that district judges adopt a more standardised inquisitorial role in small claims.

(b) The Unrepresented. The plight of the unrepresented has been well documented in socio-legal research (Dell (1971), Carlen (1976), Darbyshire (1984)). Where a defendant is unrepresented, mostly in the magistrates' courts, he is dependent on the goodwill and expertise of the Bench or, more realistically, the clerk, to help him put his case and examine witnesses and explain what is being asked of him. Some clerks are much more prepared and skilled to help than others.

The Role of the Magistrates' Clerk

When examining the role of the judge in the adversarial system, it is essential to remember to examine the peculiar role of the magistrates' clerk.

The legal position of the clerk is set down in an amalgam of case law, statute and Practice Directions. Magistrates are wholly dependent on their clerks for advice on law, practice, procedure and sentencing. The court clerk, by far the most prevalent legal adviser to magistrates, enjoyed no legal recognition whatever in this role until the enactment of section 117 of the C.L.S.A. 1990. The justices' clerk's advisory role is set out in the Justices of the Peace Act 1997, s.45. It "declares" his functions to include giving advice to justices, on request, about law, practice and procedure and empowers him to draw the magistrates' attention to these matters at any time.

As discussed above, the European Convention may require clerks to give advice in open court. There is concern over the enhancement of clerks' judicial powers of case management under the Crime and Disorder Act 1998.

The Adversarial Method of Eliciting Witnesses' Evidence

Eliciting evidence by the question and answer method. The parties are kept to a fixed order of speeches:

- (a) Prosecution or claimant makes his opening speech.
- (b) His first witness is examined by him or his legal representative. Under the CPR 1998, a witness's statement normally counts as his evidence-in-chief.

(c) This witness is then cross-examined by the opposition.
(d) Each witness is so examined until the end of the prosecution/claimant's case.
(e) Traditionally, this allowed the defendant to see the whole of the case against him, before exposing his defence which put him at an advantage. This is now massively qualified by pre-trial disclosure required by defendants tried on indictment and, in civil cases by the exchange of skeleton arguments and document bundles.
(f) The defendant is examined by the defence advocate then cross-examined by the prosecution/claimant. In civil trials, see (b) above.
(g) All the defence witnesses are so questioned.
(h) The defence sum up.
(i) The claimant/prosecution may reply.

This is meant to guarantee "fair play." In criminal trials each witness stays outside until called, so as not to copy and is kept strictly to answering the questions put. If he tries to add points he feels relevant, or pass an opinion, he is quickly stopped by the judge or advocates. This results in two things:

(i) If the witness feels he has vital evidence to add, he has no way of volunteering it. This can be especially frustrating to expert witnesses, examined by non-experts. The R.C.C.J. recommended that where expert evidence is disputed in criminal trials, the judge should invite the expert witness to say whether they wish to add to their evidence.
(ii) This system is very heavily dependent on the expertise of the advocate, to bring out all and only that relevant information helpful to his case.

The rule against leading questions. Counsel are not allowed to "lead" their own witnesses, *i.e.* ask questions which suggest an answer, unless the judge and opposition consent. The very aim of cross-examination is, however, to mislead.

THE CRIMINAL TRIAL

To call our trial accusatorial and the continental civil law system inquisitorial is a crude over simplification. Most European legal systems have incorporated the European Convention on Human Rights years ago. It requires adversarial proceedings.

Nevertheless, the defendant is provided with certain safe-guards in the criminal trial, to tip the balance slightly against the heavy weight of the State.

The Quantum of Proof

The criminal quantum of proof is proof "beyond reasonable doubt." This means that it should be more difficult for the pro-secutor to satisfy the jury or magistrates of the guilt of the defendant than it is for the claimant to satisfy the civil trial judge of a defendant's liability. The civil quantum of proof is "on the balance of probabilities." An ideal quantum of proof would con-vict all the guilty and acquit all the innocent but some error is inherent and English law prefers (at least, in theory) to err on the side of acquitting a few guilty ones, as epitomised by Black-stone: "It is better that ten guilty men go free than one innocent man should suffer." Thus, these rules are meant to protect the defendant: the quantum of proof, the fact that he sees the pro-secution case exposed first (now subject to pre-trial review in certain magistrates' courts and the C.J.P.O. Act 1994), and certain exclusory rules of evidence:

The Exclusory Rules of Evidence

Certain evidence is excluded because it is unduly prejudicial against the defendant, inherently unreliable, or its utterance is against the public interest:

(a) **Defendant's previous convictions.** But his record *is* admissible in certain circumstances.

(b) **Spouses.** Spouses are competent but not compellable for the defence but not normally competent for the prosecution.

(c) **Communications between client and legal adviser,** without permission.

(d) **Identification evidence.** Not surprising in the light of psychological findings on human memory, this is a very unreli-able type of evidence and the source of many wrongful convic-tions. It has been the subject of repeated scrutiny (*e.g.* by the *11th Report of the Criminal Law Revision Committee* (1972) and the *Devlin Committee Report* (1976)). This led to a ruling by the Court of Appeal (*R. v. Turner* (1977)) that the judge should warn the jury of the dangers of relying on it.

(e) Hearsay evidence. The basic rule against hearsay is quite simply this: evidence may not be related to the court unless its author is there to present it. It applies to both the related spoken word and to documents. It is thought to be inherently unfair to rely on the evidence of a witness who is not present to be cross-examined. Unfortunately, the hearsay rule is subject to so many exceptions that it is very difficult of application, in practice. Here are some of the exceptions:

(i) Statements of the dead, the unfit, the untraceable, etc., business documents and expert evidence, all provided for in the Criminal Justice Act 1988, ss.23–30.
(ii) Admissions or confessions.
(iii) *Res gestae*, or statements spontaneous and contemporaneous with the event (*e.g.* accusation by a victim of an attack, within minutes).
(iv) Written witness statements.

The hearsay rule in civil cases was abolished by the Civil Evidence Act 1995, following a report by the Law Commission. The R.C.C.J. recommended that hearsay be admitted to a greater degree than at present, in criminal trials, but that the rule should be examined by the Law Commission. They reported in 1995.

(f) Confessions obtained by oppression or in consequence of anything said or done which, in the circumstances, rendered the confession unreliable. The burden of proving that a confession was not so obtained is on the prosecution (Police and Criminal Evidence Act 1984, s.76). The R.C.C.J. recommended strengthening safeguards for the accused against the admission of unreliable confessions. The trial judge should be empowered to stop any case if the prosecution case is demonstrably unsafe or too weak to go to the jury. Any taped confession, unconfirmed by the accused, should be inadmissible. They recommended that the jury should be warned of the great dangers of convicting on confession evidence alone, where there is no supporting evidence. Disappointing many critics, however, the R.C.C.J. did not recommend a requirement that confession evidence be corroborated.

(g) Unfairly obtained evidence (PACE 1984, s.78).

The Right to Silence

Until The Criminal Justice And Public Order Act 1994, the defendant had an unfettered right to silence, both in the police station and in court. In court, this extended to the right not to be asked questions and the judge could comment on it but not adversely. The right was considered by the Criminal Law Revision Committee (1972), the Royal Commission on Criminal Procedure (1981) and the R.C.C.J. (1993) and it has long been a subject of controversy. The arguments about the rule go thus:

Proponents. hail it as a major (almost symbolic) safeguard of the English legal system that the defendant cannot convict himself out of his own mouth. It leaves the burden of proof entirely on the prosecution.

Opponents. say (i) it is a rule protecting the guilty (ii) it encourages the police to intimidate suspects into confessing (iii) it is sentimental to argue that the accused should not be allowed to convict himself.

Limitations Proposed. Since 1987 Conservative Home Secretaries had been considering limiting the right.

Prior to 1994, one major inroad into the right, which has wrought some criticism, was the power of the Serious Fraud Office to demand answers to certain questions, when gathering evidence. The Office had used this power frequently. In *Saunders v. United Kingdom* (E.C.H.R. 1996) the European Court of Human Rights ruled that powers exercised by the D.T.I., under the Companies Act 1985, to require a defendant to answer questions put to him pre-trial, offended against the Convention on Human Rights.

The R.C.C.J. considered the right of silence pre-trial and at trial. They recommended that the former should be retained and that only after the prosecution case had been fully disclosed should the defendant be required to answer the charges made, at the risk of adverse comment at trial on any new, undisclosed defence (an "ambush defence").

The Criminal Justice and Public Order Act 1994 goes much further than this and, critics would say, effectively abrogates both stages of the right to silence. Sections 34–39 allow the court to draw "such inferences as appear proper" from the accused's failure to mention, under police questioning, any fact which he could have been expected to mention, or failure (under questioning) to account for any objects, marks or substances, or failure (under questioning) to account for his presence at a particular place, or failure to give evidence or answer questions at trial.

5. ACCESS TO JUSTICE

If the Rule of Law states that everyone should be equal before the law then I would argue that this implies that everyone should have equal access to the law and to justice. This means, broadly: being able to make full use of legal rights, through adequate legal services, *i.e.* advice, assistance and representation, regardless of means; also, the ability to make full use of the court structure and rights of appeal.

Those issues are dealt with in this chapter and above, in relation to the adversarial process (*e.g.* Civil Justice Review).

LEGAL SERVICES FROM 2000

The Access to Justice Act 1999—Replacing Legal Aid

Civil legal aid was largely replaced, in April 2000, by the new legal services scheme, provided for in the Access to Justice Act 1999. Criminal legal aid will be replaced by criminal defence services, also provided for in the Act, in 2001. The Lord Chancellor, who is responsible for legal services, explained his plans for these schemes, in a white paper, *Modernising Justice*, which was published alongside the Access to Justice Bill, in December 1998 and in numerous consultation papers and speeches. All can be found on the L.C.D. website (*www.open.gov.uk/lcd*), under the heading "Access to Justice". Up to date detail can be found in the Legal Services Commission's publications.

The Legal Services Commission was established by section 1 of the Access to Justice Act. It consists of 7–12 members, appointed by the Lord Chancellor, according to their knowledge of social conditions, work of the courts, consumer affairs and management. Section 2 allows for replacement with two bodies, one civil, one criminal. Section 3 empowers the Commission to make contracts, loans, investments, undertake inquiries and advise the Lord Chancellor.

Community Legal Service. Section 4 requires the Commission to establish and fund a Community Legal Service to secure individual access to justice, by providing legal information, advice and help in preventing, settling or resolving disputes and enforcing decisions. The section provides that everyone involved in the C.L.S. should have regard to the desirability of promoting improvements in the range and quality of services and of achieving the swift and fair resolution of disputes. The Commission has a duty to find out about the need for and provision of services, plan what needs to be done and help other bodies to plan how to use resources to meet those needs. The Commission is empowered to set and monitor standards and provide accreditation schemes for service providers. Under section 5, the L.C. will provide the budget for the Commission to establish a Community Legal Service Fund. They must aim to secure value for money. The Commission may fund services by entering into contracts, making grants and loans, establishing bodies to provide services or themselves provide services, etc. (s.6). They may provide different services for different areas of England and Wales and the L.C. may direct them to provide particular services.

Funding code. Under section 8, the Commission must prepare a funding code, subject to the L.C.'s approval, setting out the criteria under which it is prepared to provide services and providing the form and content of applications for funding. Section 10 provides for regulations as to when recipients should pay fixed fees or contributions for legal services and section 11 provides that costs ordered against a funded individual should be kept to a reasonable amount, taking into account his resources and making allowances for his clothes, furniture and tools of trade.

Criminal Defence Service. Under section 12 the Commission must establish a Criminal Defence Service "for the purpose of securing that individuals involved in criminal investigations or criminal proceedings have access to such advice, assistance and representation as the interests of justice require". (Effectively, this means cases will only be funded if required "in the interests of Justice". This test is identical to the old merits test for criminal legal aid. Trivial cases will not be funded.) It can set up an accreditation and monitoring scheme and fund such advice and assistance as it considers appropriate, by making contracts, grants, loans or establishing and maintaining advice and assistance bodies, or employing people to provide advice and assistance. It can fund advice and assistance by different means in different areas of England and Wales. (s. 13) Under section 14, it has a duty to fund representation in criminal cases to people who have been granted a right to it under the Act. Section 15 provides that the represented individual may select any representative to act for him but it may be from a prescribed group but regulations may not provide that only a person employed by the Commission or a body maintained by the Commission may be selected. Under Section 16, the Commission must prepare a code of conduct for its employees and funded providers which includes a duty of non-discrimination and duties to the court, etc. Under section 17, where anyone is represented in a criminal court other than a magistrates' court, the court may ask them to pay for some or all of their representation. Under Schedule 3, the criminal courts are empowered to grant representation.

Conditional Fee Arrangements. Under Part II of the Act, headed "Other Funding of Legal Services", conditional fee agreements, as provided for by the Courts and Legal Services Act 1990, are defined, in section 58(2) as "an agreement with a person providing advocacy or litigation services which provides for his fee and expenses, or any part of them, to be payable only in specified circumstances". (Of course the specified circumstances normally mean a success fee is paid only if the lawyer wins the case.) Conditions are prescribed: agreements must be in writing, must satisfy regulations and must relate to proceedings specified by the Lord Chancellor. They are prohibited in relation to criminal proceedings and virtually all family proceedings. Section 29 provides that insurance premiums for policies insuring against the risk of losing the case may be recovered in costs awarded by the court.

Legal Services Consultative Panel. Section 35 abolishes ACLEC, the Lord Chancellor's previous advisory committee. The

L.C. had criticised the body in his paper on the right of audience. He thought it had too many people, cost too much (£1 million p.a.) and had succeeded in obstructing rather than furthering the statutory objective of the Courts and Legal Services Act 1990, to open up competition in the provision of legal services. It is replaced with a small Legal Services Consultative Panel, appointed by the L.C., with "the duty of assisting in the maintenance and development of standards in the education, training and conduct of persons offering legal services by considering relevant issues in accordance with a programme of work approved by the Lord Chancellor and, where the Consultative Panel considers it appropriate to do so, making recommendations to him". They are obliged to advise the L.C. when he calls on them.

Rights of audience Section 36–48 are one of the most provocative bits of the Act but the most exciting for all lawyers who are not practising barristers, because they open up rights of audience to employed barristers and to solicitors. They stem from the L.C.'s frustration at the lack of progress in opening up rights of audience, one of the stated aims of the Courts and Legal Services Act 1990. This reform is explained earlier in this book, in the section on lawyers.

Modernising Justice (White Paper, December 1998) explains the Government's plans to radically overhaul legal services. Chapters 2, 3 and 6 cover legal aid and legal services. The Government had identified these problems, in the old legal aid scheme:

- inadequate access to quality information—poor co-ordination in services.
- inability to control and target legal aid.
- restrictive practices and cumbersome court procedures. They intended to replace legal aid with a community legal service.

The legal advice sector had grown randomly. The C.L.S. would:

- develop a system for assessing needs and priorities and monitoring standards
- co-ordinate plans of various funders

- treat the advice sector and advice by lawyers under one budget

A new Legal Services Commission would:

- develop broad, regional and national plans to match provision to needs
- report annually to the L.C.
- manage C.L.S. funds, which will replace legal aid in civil and family cases
- make contracts, fund traditional or other types of provider
- take account of local views
- develop partnerships with local authorities, etc.

The interim project in 1999 was to:

- develop systems for assessing need
- develop core quality criteria
- build a C.L.S. website on legal advice
- launch four pioneer partnerships

The Legal Services Commission would develop a quality system by

- integrating it with the existing franchising system
- kitemarking non-lawyers

As for the legal profession, the Government would

- cut restrictive practices
- improve standards
- make legal services more affordable through:
  — legal insurance
  — regulating cost
  — expanding provision for conditional fees.

Chapter 6 on criminal defence said the Government's objectives were to

- ensure a fair hearing, by putting the defendant on an equal footing with the prosecution
- protect interest of the defendant

- maintain the defendant's confidence and effective participation.

The Criminal Defence Service must reflect domestic law (PACE) and international law (art. 6 of the European Convention on Human Rights). The Government said weaknesses of the present system were:

- cost
- the lawyers' pay framework was outdated because of:
  — inappropriate financial incentives
  — a few disproportionately expensive cases
- the means test was flawed: note that the Lord Chancellor has scrapped any requirement for the recipient of criminal defence services to pay for some or all of his legal services, except that a Crown Court judge may order a defendant to pay some or all of the costs of representation. The L.C. scrapped the means test because magistrates' clerks were so bad at administering the legal aid means tests and were castigated by the Public Accounts Committee for squandering legal aid money for the last seven years.
- the legal aid scheme was highly fragmented.

Fundamental reform was necessary. Legal aid would be replaced with a Criminal Defence Service. It would:

- be separate from C.L.S., with a separate budget
- but both run by the Legal Services Commission
- cover all services provided under legal aid
- develop more efficient ways of proceduring services, through:
  — contracts with accredited private practice lawyers, replacing franchising.
  — salaried defenders on the model piloted in Scotland.
  — restricting client choice to a duty solicitor or accredited solicitor.
- abolish means testing, targeting rich defendants.
- in 1999, establish pilot contracts for representation in youth courts.

The Legal Services Commission replaced the Legal Aid Board in April 2000 (*www.legalservices.gov.uk*).

Developing the New Legal Services Model

The Legal Services Consultative Panel provided its first advice to the Lord Chancellor, on proposed changes to rights of audience, in April 2000.

Thirteen Regional Legal Service Committees were established in 1997–98 and published their *Assessment of Need for Legal Services* by July 1999. They had organised their priorities. They identified particular groups suffering from an unmet need for legal services: those living in rural areas, the elderly, people with mental health problems, people whose first language was not English and those appearing before employment tribunals.

The New System for Civil Cases

The Community Legal Service. In May 1999, the Government published a consultation paper on how they would develop this institution. (L.C.D. website). It made the following points:

- People need basic information and advice on rights and responsibilities, not necessarily to go to court.
- 6,000 professionals (lawyers) and 30,000 volunteers at Law Centres and other advice centres, such as Citizen's Advice Bureaux, etc., provide this for £250 million per year. (By March 2000, the junior minister said their estimate was that about a billion pounds per year was spent on legal services.)
- This is enough but service is fragmented and uncoordinated.
- The Legal Services Commission is the new coordinating body. It will take over and develop the Legal Aid Board's responsibilities.
- It will work in "Community Legal Service partnerships", targeting funds to local needs.

In the meantime,

- pioneer partnerships were developed in six local authority areas, in 1999, bringing together the local authority, Legal Aid Board and local providers of legal services.

- The core criteria were developed for the legal service providers' quality mark
- A legal services website was being developed. (Comment: *Guardian* research in 1999 showed only 2 per cent of social classes D and E are online.)

The paper gave case studies demonstrating how difficult it was for people with certain problems to obtain satisfactory advice. The lack of an effective referral network meant people got initial advice and were sent away so the new legal services network should include:

- lawyers
- professionals outside private practice
- advice workers
- para-legals with specialist knowledge, *e.g.* Trading Standards Officers
- volunteers in Citizens' Advice Bureaux, etc.

The C.L.S. should provide information, advice and assistance. Need for legal service varies geographically. Research showed no area where strategy had been developed jointly by different funders. Time was wasted by advice agencies demonstrating the quality of their services to their different funders, *e.g.* one Asian women's group had 10 funders and 40 per cent of its manager's time was spent on reporting to them. Quantifying need was difficult. Statistics indicated unmet need for legal services resulted not from inadequate provision but from "lack of access to appropriate adequate help of adequate quality".

The C.L.S. was officially launched in April, replacing the Legal Aid Board. One of its first acts was to deliver to every home in Cornwall (one of the pioneers) an information card on how to get good legal advice. This would be extended nationwide. The C.L.S. funds replaced the previous civil and family legal aid budget.

Contracting. The introduction of general civil contracting brought a massive shift in funding of legal services. Whereas any solicitor could apply to give legally aided services but few non-solicitor agencies could, providers of legal help are now limited to those who have a contract with the Legal Services Commission to deal with a specified number of cases. To get this, an advice agency or firm of solicitors must demonstrate they satisfy the quality criteria, *e.g.* they need to show that they have a satisfactory management system, that staff work is closely supervised and they had to have computerised systems by August 2000. The predecessor to this was the franchising system, introduced by the last Government by about 1994, whereby providers could get a franchise to provide services from the Legal Aid Board but did not have to do so. Franchised firms and agencies were already subject to rigorous quality criteria and auditing so became the first contracted providers. A provider may have a general civil contract, a family contract, if on the family panel, or a controlled work contract, in areas such as immigration, mental health, community care, public law and actions against the police. Every contracted supplier gets regular payments based on regular reports to the Legal Services Commission. Their work is audited by inspection of sample files. Contractors can call specialist phone lines for help in advising clients. The first barristers' chambers to be awarded a contract for advice and representation in employment, immigration and housing law was 2 Garden Court.

The Funding Code was launched at the same time, having been approved by Parliament. It replaced the old civil merits test for legal aid. It provides seven levels of service, which may be provided in different ways and may attract different eligibility and remuneration.

- legal help
- help at court (these replace the old legal advice and assistance, under the legal aid scheme)
- approved family help (general help or mediation)
- legal representation (investigative help or full representation)
- support funding (either investigative or litigation support)
- family mediation
- such other services as are authorized by the Lord Chancellor.

Legal help, help at court and certain types of representation are classified as controlled work and can only be carried out by lawyers or legal advisers with a general civil contract (a contract with the Legal Services Commission as an accredited provider). These providers are fully responsible for granting and withdrawing help in these cases. Funding for most cases requiring representation, approved family help and support funding will be granted by a certificate awarded by the Commission. Eight categories of service are excluded:

- personal injury, apart from clinical negligence
- conveyancing
- boundary disputes
- wills
- trust law
- defamation
- company or partnership law
- other business matters.

The Lord Chancellor announced the *priorities* of the new C.L.S., such as public law, mental health, community care and asylum seekers. Note that funding is now provided for representation before the immigration adjudicators and the immigration appeal tribunal, whereas legal aid had not been available. He set up a specific budget for very high cost cases. Personal injuries, for which legal aid had been available, were removed from the scheme because the Government thinks that most of those cases can be funded through conditional fee agreements. Clinical negligence cases and actions against the police for tort remain within scope of the new fund. The only A.D.R. specifically provided for is mediation but this is likely to be extended and will generally now be funded under legal help or representation. Arbitration can be funded, whereas it could not have been provided under the legal aid scheme. The *prospects of success* are evaluated for those clients applying for funding for representation. This means the likelihood of a successful outcome in the proceedings. Generally, at least a 50 per cent prospect of success is required but funding may be granted to borderline cases if, for example, the case has overwhelming importance to the client, has a wider public interest, is a human rights judicial review, involves housing possession, domestic violence or children. The Code provides various cost benefit tests, which usually mean comparing likely cost with likely damages obtainable.

Financial eligibility limits are updated by regulations, every April, as were the old legal aid means tests. Only clients with very low incomes and capital are entitled to fully funded legal services. Those whose income or capital fall above certain limits will have to pay a contribution towards certain (but not all) legal services, assessed according to means.

Conditional fee agreements. Legal representation or investigative help will not be granted in cases suitable for conditional fee agreements. A conditional fee agreement means, for example, a no-win, no-fee contract or a contract whereby the lawyer gets a higher fee if he wins the case. Distinguish it from a *contingency fee agreement* which is illegal here but well known in the United States, whereby the lawyer takes a percentage of any damages won. Conditional fees were permitted by the Courts and Legal Services Act 1990 but widened in scope in April 2000, when three sets of rules came into force providing the new framework for conditional fee agreements. It applies to all civil proceedings except specified family proceedings. The maximum success fee which can be contracted for is 100 per cent.

The Quality Mark was launched on the same day. It is a symbol which the accredited quality providers are allowed to display. This includes over 6,000 solicitors' offices, Citizens' Advice Bureaux and other advice centres.

Just ask! The C.L.S. website was launched in April 2000, *www.justask.org.uk*, providing a directory of legal services.

C.L.S. partnerships. By October 2000, 142 had been formed, involving 265 local authorities, the aim being to cover the whole of England and Wales by 2002.

The New System in Criminal Cases

In 2000, the Government published two consultation papers on the Criminal Defence Service, which will be launched in April 2001 (see L.C.D. website). They propose to develop a system of public defenders directly employed by the Legal Services Commission but clients will generally be able to choose between them and any private practice lawyer, except in cases like serious fraud, where they would be limited to specially qualified lawyers.

From October 2000, all solicitors firms undertaking publicly funded criminal defence work will have to have a franchise (contract) with the C.D.S. A serious fraud panel was established in May 2000.

In July 2000, the Lord Chancellor announced he would reduce fees for criminal defence lawyers, to reduce the disparity between fees paid to prosecutors and defence lawyers.

Background to the Reforms—Why Was Legal Aid Scrapped?

Throughout the 1990s, both the Conservative government then their Labour successor were seriously concerned that something radical had to be done to reform the provision of legal services. Why?

- *The cost* was "spiralling out of control", according to the Conservative Lord Chancellor, Lord Mackay. Legal aid was the only demand led draw on the Treasury. Some years in the 1990s the cost rose by around 20 per cent, despite the fact that fewer people were being legally aided. The Children Act 1989, providing separate representation for children and the development of duty solicitor schemes in police stations and the magistrates' courts were items which accelerated the cost increase and the public were concerned that a few cases cost millions of pounds when apparently wealthy defendants, such as the Maxwells, were legally aided.
- *Unmet legal need* was identified by research in the 1970s. It means that where someone has a problem which could be remedied by use of the law, that problem remains unsolved through lack of legal help. It was caused by

  - the high cost of legal fees
  - fear of lawyers, fear of cost
  - lawyers' lack of training and unwillingness to serve poor client's needs for advice in welfare law
  - the inaccessibility of lawyers' offices to poor or rural clients
  - the creation of new legal rights without the funding to enforce them
  - people's ignorance that the law could solve their problem
  - the fact that the legal aid scheme omitted certain services, such as representation at tribunals.
- *Funders were uncoordinated.* Legal aid was designed to deliver legal services through the medium of private

practice barristers and solicitors so alternative legal services, listed below, received very little of the huge budget and they were dependent on a precarious mix of sources, such as charities, local authorities and other Government departments.

- *Criminal legal aid was administered unevenly.* Research showed that the "Widgery criteria", merits test was applied differently between magistrates' courts and the Audit Commission criticised them eight years running for failing to apply the means test properly. Fat cat lawyers, as the present Lord Chancellor calls them, were charging the Legal Aid Board exorbitant fees.

In 1999, Hazell Genn published the most modern survey of how people solve their legal problems: *Paths to Justice*, summarised at (1999) 149 N.L.J. 1756. She found that people were generally extraordinarily ignorant about their legal rights and obligations.

Comment: the present government's scheme was quite visionary. It was first announced in the Labour party policy paper, *Access to Justice*, in 1995. They had the simple idea of finding out how much money was spent on legal services in England and Wales and working out what legal needs were and how they could best be fulfilled, whether through private practice lawyers or alternatives.

"Alternative" Legal Services

Because the shortcomings of the legal aid scheme and the causes of unmet legal need were identified since the 1970s, alternatives to private practice were developed to try to meet that need. These can no longer be seen as alternatives because they have just been absorbed into mainstream state regulated provision and C.L.S. funding. Lord Chief Justice Bingham gave a neat list of these alternatives in the Barnett Lecture in 1998 (L.C.D. website):

- *53 Law Centres*, deliberately established in poor areas, with a shop front image, where employed lawyers and para-legals provide advice and representation on such matters as welfare law and immigration. They were established since 1973 but have always suffered from vulnerable funding. Those financed by local authorities found they were biting the hand that fed them, when they acted for groups suffering bad public housing. Law centre funding was sporadic and sometimes they would have to close temporarily.

- *700 Citizens' Advice Bureaux.*
- *800 independent advice centres*, covering diverse areas, sometimes providing legal services themselves and sometimes making referrals. Examples are the Child Poverty Action Group, Shelter, Youth Access, the Money Advice Association, Dial U.K. (disability advice), Mind, the Refugee Legal Centre, etc. Lawyers often provide advice free at evening advice centres but would need to make a referral if substantive legal help was needed.
- *Pro-Bono* groups of both solicitors and barristers, newly organised in the 1990s, where professionals pledge to give their service free to some clients. The *Free Representation Unit*, a group of Bar students prepared to represent claimants in appearances before tribunals, etc., was established in the 1970s.

In addition, the Conservative administrations of the 1990s had devised various other ways of enhancing access to justice, which have been expanded under the new scheme:

- Conditional fees, as described above but in a limited sphere.
- Simplifying the law (plain English) and making court procedures simpler and cheaper and providing good advice leaflets and a Citizens' Advice Bureaux in the Royal Courts of Justice to help people represent themselves.
- Encouraging A.D.R, the cheaper and quicker resolution of disputes, out of court.
- Encouraging private legal expenses insurance.
- Duty solicitors, funded under the legal aid scheme, to provide emergency help and representation in police stations and the magistrates' courts.

Criticism of the New Scheme

- *Conditional fees.* When the Lord Chancellor announced he was abolishing most civil legal aid, leaving people to rely on conditional funding agreements there was uproar

among the legal profession. The criticisms were too pro-
lific to summarise here. The profession argued it would
be a straight denial of justice, often pointing to specific
clients, such as victims of police brutality or clinical negligence. The Lord Chancellor has had to make a lengthy
list of concessions, providing services for all those groups
listed above.

- *Contracting/franchising.* Again, this provoked condemna-
  tion from private practice lawyers who said that limiting
  providers to those who won contracts would exclude
  many firms of solicitors, such as small ethnic minority
  practices. This would deprive the public of access to justice, as firms turned them away. Complaints are now
  being made that this prediction has become a reality (*The
  Times*, July 4, 2000).
- *Tribunals.* Only five types qualify for publicly funded representation and the criticism continues that applicants
  suffer injustice through a lack of representation.
- *Astonishingly, the new Civil Justice Council* attacked the
  plan for the C.L.S. in 1999.
- *Rationing.* Michael Zander and other critics have accused
  the Lord Chancellor of being motivated purely by cost
  cutting.
- *Public defenders.* U.K. lawyers are well aware of the image
  of the American public defender providing a second class
  service to criminal clients.

APPEALS

Criminal Appeals

Appeals from the Magistrates' Court.

1. Appeals to the Crown Court. A defendant may appeal,
as of right, on fact or law and against sentence and/or conviction. The appeal is a complete rehearing by a circuit judge and
two to four magistrates.

The Crown Court may:

(i) correct any mistake in the order or judgment,
(ii) confirm, reverse or vary the decision,
(iii) remit the matter, with their opinion, to the magistrates,
(iv) make any order they think just and exercise any power of

the magistrates' court. Thus, they may increase sentence, within the magistrates' maxima.

2. Appeals to the High Court by way of case stated. Any prosecutor or defendant, aggrieved by the magistrates' decision, may, if they consider it wrong in law or in excess of jurisdiction, apply to the magistrates to state a case for the opinion of the High Court.

The stated case is a statement of reasons for the decision drafted by the magistrates' clerk.

These appeals are heard by the Divisional Court of the QBD who may:

    (i) reverse, affirm or amend the decision;
   (ii) remit it to the magistrates, with an opinion;
  (iii) make such other orders as they think fit, including directing the magistrates to convict or acquit. (Note: this is the only instance where a prosecutor can appeal to reverse an acquittal.)

Appeals from the Crown Court to the Court of Appeal (Criminal Division).

1. Appeal against conviction. Under the Criminal Appeal Act 1995, s.1, the convicted defendant may appeal if he has either a certificate from the trial judge that the case is fit for appeal or if leave of the Court of Appeal is obtained. Single High Court judges consider written applications for leave. Applicants have around a 25 per cent chance of success. Where leave is refused, the judge may order that time spent in custody after lodging the appeal should not count towards sentence. This is to discourage frivolous appeals, which burden the lists and delay meritorious appeals.

The Court of Appeals's powers are set out in the Criminal Appeal Act 1968, which has been substantially amended by the Criminal Appeal Act 1995. I will set out the amended version of the 1968 Act and then explain the background to the 1995 Act.

The Power of the Court of Appeal to Admit Fresh Evidence.

Under section 23(1) and (3) of the 1968 Act, as amended by the 1995 Act, the CA *may*, "if they think it necessary or expedient in the interests of justice"

(a) order the production of any document, exhibit or other thing connected with the proceedings;

(b) order the examination of any witness who would have been a compellable witness at the trial, whether or not he or she was called; and

(c) receive any evidence which was not adduced in the proceedings from which the appeal lies.

In considering whether to receive evidence, the CA must have regard in particular to:

"(a) whether the evidence appears to the court to be capable of belief;

(b) whether it appears to the court that the evidence may afford any ground for allowing the appeal;

(c) whether the evidence would have been admissible in the proceedings from which the appeal lies on an issue which is the subject of the appeal; and

(d) whether there is a reasonable explanation for the failure to adduce the evidence in those proceedings" (1968 Act, s.23 (2), as substituted by section 4 of the 1995 Act).

Background

Under the old law (1968 Act until 1995), the CA had a duty to admit fresh evidence where it was not available at the original trial but a wider power to admit it "if they think it necessary or expedient in the interests of justice" (1968 Act, s.23). Several points arise:

(a) The Court of Appeal's strict approach was shown by these cases:

R. v. Flower (CA, 1965). Widgery J. said it was the duty of the court to consider and assess the reliability of witnesses and the court could then take one of three views:

(i) If satisfied that the fresh evidence was true and conclusive, the court would normally quash the conviction but, if not conclusive, order a retrial.

(ii) If not satisfied that the fresh evidence is true but nevertheless thinks it might be acceptable to a jury, the court would normally order a retrial.

(iii) If they disbelieve the evidence, they will disregard it;

but in *Stafford v. D.P.P.* (HL 1974) Viscount Dilhorne added that, if the court was satisfied that there was no reasonable doubt about the guilt of the accused, the conviction should not be quashed even though the jury might have come to a different view. The court was not bound to ask whether the evidence might have led to the jury returning a verdict of not guilty.

(b) This approach was criticised by Lord Devlin, who argued it was wrong, in principle, for judges rather than juries to decide whether the appellant was guilty. Where fresh evidence *could* have made a difference, the proper course would be for the court to order a new trial. The first verdict should be regarded as unsatisfactory simply because the original jury did not see all the evidence.

(c) The reluctance of the Court of Appeal to admit fresh evidence was repeatedly criticised by the pressure group, JUSTICE and by the producers of the television series *Rough Justice* and authors of the book of the same name, all of which focused on alleged miscarriages of justice which resulted in wrongful imprisonment.

The cases they highlighted and similar, highly publicised ones showed that the Court of Appeal required a particular type of explanation why evidence was not called at the time of trial, such as that it was *not available*. If it was available but simply not called, owing to, say, defence lawyers' negligence, prosecution's obstructiveness or a shortfall of legal aid, then this apparently would not suffice as an explanation acceptable to the Court of Appeal. In many of these cases it took a "trial by television" and a reference by the Home Secretary to re-open the case. It appears, then, that the Court of Appeal was restricting its open *discretion* under the 1968 Act, s.23(1) and (3) by the criteria of s.23(2) (see above) which invoke the *duty* to admit fresh evidence. It was thus alleged to be perpetrating injustices by an over-reluctance to operate its discretion.

As public concern about miscarriages of justice reached a crescendo in the early 1980s, the House of Commons Home Affairs Committee produced a report entitled *Miscarriages of Justice* (see below). In its White Paper reply, the Government gave the following reassurance:

"The Lord Chief Justice ... sees room for the Court to be more ready to exercise its own powers to receive evidence or, where appropriate and practicable, to order a retrial ... The Lord Chief Justice has confirmed that the Court of Appeal is very ready to use its discretion to admit new evidence, under section 23 of the Criminal Appeal Act 1968, when the interests of justice so require."

Nevertheless, JUSTICE reported, in its 1989 publication *Miscarriages of Justice*, that practice had not noticeably changed. The Royal Commission on Criminal Justice, in 1993 again urged the CA to take a broad approach to the question whether fresh evidence was available at the time of the trial and, if it were, to the explanation why it was not adduced or why a witness had changed her story. The test for receiving fresh evidence should be whether it was "capable of belief." In fresh evidence cases, the CA should order a retrial unless impracticable, in which case they should decide the case themselves.

In their responding 1994 consultation paper, the Home Office broadly agreed but thought the CA's power to exclude fresh evidence should be preserved, in cases where there was no reasonable explanation for the failure to produce it at trial. As you can see, this is satisfied in the Act by the use of the word *may* in conjunction with their power to have regard to the explanation offered.

Grounds for Allowing and Dismissing Appeals. Section 2 of the Criminal Appeal Act 1968, as amended by the 1995 Act, now provides that:

"Subject to the provisions of this Act, the Court of Appeal
  (a) shall allow an appeal against conviction if they think that the conviction is unsafe; and
  (b) shall dismiss such an appeal in any other case."

Background. Under the un-amended Act, the Court had the power to allow an appeal if they thought a jury's verdict "unsafe or unsatisfactory" or that there was an error of law or material irregularity in the course of the trial. Section 2 included a very important "proviso" which meant that the Court could dismiss an appeal where, despite finding that something had gone wrong at the trial, they thought the defendant was, nevertheless, really guilty so that "no miscarriage of justice has actually occurred". The CA had been criticised for too readily using the proviso to uphold convictions where something had gone seriously wrong at the trial.

The R.C.C.J. recommended that section 2(1) of the 1968 Act should be redrafted. They considered that the grounds overlapped and that there was confusion over the proviso. The grounds, they recommended, should be replaced by a single broad ground, giving the CA power to rule in any case where it felt a conviction "is or may be unsafe." The proviso would be redundant if the CA simply dismissed an appeal where they found an error had not rendered a conviction unsafe or ordered a retrial in those cases where it considered a conviction may be unsafe. This power would be exercisable regardless of there being no fresh evidence, no error in law and no material irregularity.

The CA should have an additional power to refer cases that require further investigation to a new body to be responsible for investigating alleged miscarriages of justice.

The Government broadly agreed with these proposals in its 1994 Home Office consultation paper, *Criminal Appeals and the Establishment of A Criminal Cases Review Authority* but notice that the CA now has to be satisfied that the verdict is unsafe. The Commission's words "or may be" have not been included in the section. Critics have said that this is too restrictive on the CA's powers. Although the proviso is now abolished, the court's new powers may have the same effect.

As well as the power to quash a conviction, the Court also has the power to order a retrial (discussed below) or convict for an alternative offence, or substitute a verdict of insanity or unfitness to plead.

The Court of Appeal's attitude towards its powers. Generally speaking, the CA was criticised for placing too restrictive an interpretation on its already limited powers. Prior to 1995, section 2 had been interpreted by Widgery L.J. in *R. v. Cooper* (CA, 1969) as requiring the CA judges to ask themselves the substantive question "whether there is not some lurking doubt in our minds, which makes us wonder whether an injustice has been done." The R.C.C.J. thought the Court should be less reluctant to use its powers to overturn jury verdicts but the Home Secretary and the judges, at the time of the passage of the 1995 Act, said the new version of section 2 simply restates the Court's previous practice. The main reason why the CA is so reluctant to overturn a conviction by a jury is that, unlike the jury, they have not seen the witnesses and evidence first-hand. Further, they tend to revere the primacy of the jury, as the quotation below illustrates.

It is important to understand that the CA does not provide a rehearing in criminal cases, unlike an appeal from a magistrates' court to the Crown Court. The limited powers of the CA were spelled out in the successful appeal of the Birmingham Six, in 1991, *R. v. McIlkenny and ors*, in a judgment read out by the judges in turn:

> "Nothing in s.2 of the Act, or anywhere else obliges or entitles us to say whether we think that the appellant is innocent. This is a point of great constitutional importance. The task of deciding whether a man is innocent or guilty falls on the jury. We are concerned solely with the question whether the verdict of the jury can stand.
>
> Rightly or wrongly (we think rightly) trial by jury is the foundation of our criminal justice system. . . . The primacy of the jury in the criminal justice system is well illustrated by the difference between the Criminal and Civil Divisions of the Court of Appeal. . . . A civil appeal is by way of rehearing of the whole case. So the court is concerned with fact as well as law. . . . It follows that in a civil case the Court of Appeal may take a different view of the facts from the court below. In a criminal case this is not possible . . . the Criminal Division is perhaps more accurately described as a court of review."

The Power to order retrials. The 1968 Act, s.7, as amended by the Criminal Justice Act 1988, provides that, where the CA allows an appeal against convinction, it may order that the appellant be retried where it appears that this is required in the interests of justice.

Background. Prior to the 1988 amendment, the CA could only order a retrial where it had admitted fresh evidence. Some critics say the amendment does not go far enough and that the CA should have been given a wider power, as exists in Scotland.

Justice considered whether the Court of Appeal should have unlimited power to order retrials, following appeals from conviction. They found opinions so divided that they published both sides' views, which can be summarised as follows:

Anti-retrials

(a) Absence of a general power of retrial ensures the accused cannot be subjected to a second ordeal.

(b) Statistics show a new general power would be used infrequently.

(c) Most cases where the Court of Appeal has complained of a lack of power to order retrial are cases where they have allowed an appeal. There is no reason why the judicial system should be allowed a second attempt to provide a fair trial.

(d) There is no evidence that retrial would replace some dismissals of appeal.

(e) There are real doubts as to the fairness of a second trial. The second jury may well now know of the defendant's record and have noted other adverse publicity, as well as knowing that the defendant has been convicted.

(f) Practitioners dislike new trials because the evidence is stale and cross-examination cannot be successful.

(g) Experience from abroad is adverse.

(h) Those pro-retrial recommend only one retrial. There can be no logical reason for this so they impliedly admit to the oppressiveness of retrial.

Pro-retrials

(a) A general power to order retrial would assist in acquitting the innocent and convicting the guilty.

(b) The majority of wrongful convictions result from mistaken identify. This will not be quashed by the Court of Appeal but they might order retrials if they could.

As stated above, the 1988 Act extends the power of retrial. A useful analysis is made by Alldridge (1987) 137 N.L.J. 1189.

The R.C.C.J. favoured retrials where possible. In cases without fresh evidence, where a retrial was desirable but impracticable, the CA, they recommended, should automatically allow an appeal. In fresh evidence cases, they should decide the appeal themselves only if a retrial were impracticable. The Home Office, in its response, disagreed with the first recommendation, preferring that the CA decide these cases itself.

Appeals against Sentence. The defendant may appeal from the Crown Court to the CA, who may substitute any other sentence or order within the powers of the Crown Court, provided it is not more severe than originally. The Criminal Justice Act 1988, s. 36 gives the Attorney-General a prosecutorial power to refer any "unduly lenient" Crown Court sentence to the CA, who then have the power to increase it. The Attorney may then refer any such decision of the CA to the House of Lords.

Attorney-General's References. The Attorney may, under the Criminal Justice Act 1972, refer an appeal, following an acquittal, to the CA and HL, on behalf of the prosecution. The appeal court simply clarifies the law, leaving the acquittal untouched.

Appeals to the House of Lords.

1. Appeals from the High Court ("leapfrog" appeals). Either prosecutor or defendant may appeal, with leave, to the House of Lords, from an appeal hearing in the Divisional Court, on a point of law of general public importance. (Administration of Justice Act 1960.)

2. Appeals from the Court of Appeal. Either prosecutor or defendant may appeal, provided the Court of Appeal certifies that a point of law of general public importance is involved and that either court considers that the point should be considered by the House and grants leave. The House, in disposing of the appeal, may exercise any of the powers of the Court of Appeal, or remit the case to it. (Criminal Appeal Act 1968.)

The Post Appeal Stage: Re-examining Alleged Miscarriages of Justice.

Where a person thinks he has been wrongly convicted by a jury or magistrates and he has lost an appeal or been refused leave to appeal, he may now seek the assistance of the newly created Criminal Cases Review Commission or somebody else may petition them on his behalf. (Judging from the past, this is likely to be an M.P. or a campaigning group, or an organisation such as JUSTICE). It was created by Part II of the 1995 Act and started work in 1997. It is a body corporate, independent of the Crown. Its 11 members are appointed for terms of five years. At least one third must be legally qualified. The Commission is empowered to refer Crown Court convictions and sentences to the Court of Appeal and summary convictions and sentences to the Crown Court. The Commission must "consider that there is a real possibility that the conviction, verdict, finding or sentence would not be upheld, were the reference to be made" because of argument or evidence not raised earlier. These conditions appear rather restrictive but these are followed by a broad power to make a reference "if it appears to the Commission that there are exceptional circumstances which justify making it."

The Commission may be directed by the Court of Appeal to investigate a case and may be asked by the Home Secretary to consider a matter arising in his consideration of whether to exercise the prerogative of mercy. The Commission has powers to obtain documents and may direct investigations by police officers or another public body.

Although the Commission is a welcome replacement for the former arrangements for investigating miscarriages of justice, the statute has been criticised for not providing the body with independent investigators and concern has been expressed that its first chairman is a senior freemason.

Background. Prior to 1995, the Home Secretary had both a prerogative power of mercy, which he retains, and a statutory power, under section 17 of the 1968 Act, to refer cases to the CA. Constitutionally, the Home Secretary has always used the prerogative to pardon sparingly, so as not to invoke the criticism of over-interference of the executive in the judicial function and because of the notion that the jury's verdict is sacrosanct. The House of Commons Home Affairs Committee complained in 1981 that the prerogative was used reluctantly, that decisions of vital importance to the liberty of the individual were taken anonymously by civil servants, after unexplained delays and with no reasons given for a complainant's rejection. They recommended an independent review body to advise on the exercise of the prerogative, rendering the use of referrals under section 17 redundant. In its White Paper reply, however, the Government rejected these proposals, on the constitutional grounds mentioned above but gave the assurance that the Home Secretary would be more ready to refer cases to the Court of Appeal and that Home Office procedures in dealing with petitions for the prerogative would be reviewed. In its 1989 publication, *Miscarriages of Justice*, however (see below), JUSTICE reported that there had been fewer references per year since this assurance was given, not more.

The R.C.C.J. proposed that the Home Secretary's power under section 17 be replaced by a new authority, along the lines of that now created. The Home Office responded, in a 1994 consultation paper, expanding on the Royal Commission's recommendations. They drew attention to the difficult constitutional issues involved in establishing the relationship between the Authority and the Court of Appeal, such as the need to prevent the Authority from usurping the courts's functions.

The royal prerogative of mercy. The prerogative of mercy is the power to pardon convicted individuals as part of the residuary royal prerogative, exercised by the Crown on the advice of the Home Secretary, effectively, by civil servants. The prerogative is exercised in three ways:

(a) A free pardon: quashing and expunging a conviction.
(b) A conditional pardon: excusing or varying the conviction, subject to conditions, *e.g.* by commuting sentences.
(c) Remission of a sentence.

General Background to the Criminal Appeal Act 1995— Widespread Concern Over Miscarriages of Justice

The most famous miscarriages of justice in modern times were the cases of the Guildford Four and the Birmingham Six. The R.C.C.J. was established on the day the latter were released, in 1991, to investigate the criminal justice process. Concerns had, however, been raised for decades beforehand, over individuals who had allegedly been wrongfully imprisoned. Television programmes such as *Rough Justice* had alerted the public to the inadequacy of the appeal and post-appeal procedures. These are probably best summarised in a JUSTICE Report, *Miscarriages of Justice, 1989* known as *The Waller Report*. It is well worth reading and, below, I list the causes of injustice identified by their report, explaining, in square brackets, how these were later manifested in these famous cases:

Pre-Trial

a. Poor work by defence lawyers.
b. Cases involving poor police investigation and/or police misconduct. [The stories behind the Guildford Four and Birmingham Six involve a sad litany of police corruption, notably of police brutality inducing false confessions.] The Report recites psychiatric research which gives a fas-

cinating insight into why people confess to crimes they
did not commit.

Trial

   c. Poor work by defence counsel: late briefs, bad trial tactics
and failure to call witnesses.

   d. Underhand tactics by the prosecution. [In the Guildford
Four case, it was alleged that the police realised, early on,
that they might not have caught the right people but they
suppressed evidence in favour of the defence, such as an
interview with an alibi witness.]

   e. Poor summing up by the judge. [In the Guildford Four
case, the summing up by the trial judge was acknowledged by the Court of Appeal to be faulty but they did
not consider it sufficient reason to allow leave to appeal.
As for the Birmingham Six, the summing up by their trial
judge (who later became a Law Lord) went overboard in
indicating a guilty verdict.]

Appeal

   f. bad advice on appeal.

   g. The majority of appeals are concerned with legal technic-
alities, not the guilt or innocence of the accused.

   h. A reluctance to interfere with the trial verdict. [In the
Birmingham Six case, the Court of Appeal, headed by
Lord Lane C.J., which heard the Six's 1987 appeal, was
very heavily criticised for its refusal to overturn the jury's
verdict, despite new evidence casting serious doubt on
the convictions.]

Post-Appeal

   i. The desire of the Home Secretary, as part of the executive,
not to be seen to be interfering with the work of the courts
leads him to ignore errors under a. to g. [By the time the
Home Secretary had referred the Birmingham Six's
appeal back to the Court of Appeal, the case had already
been the subject of a book and a T.V. drama documentary
and opinion polls showed that most Americans, including President Bush and most Irish people, including their
Prime Minister, assumed the Six to be innocent.]

j. Inadequate re-investigation by the police. [The police were criticised for taking two years to investigate the Guildford Four's convictions.]

Additionally, the above cases highlighted specific weaknesses in the system:

k. Inefficiency in forensic science services and inadequate services for the defence, as emphasised by the May inquiry into the Guildford and Maguire cases.

l. Inadequate safeguards for defendants held under the Prevention of Terrorism Act. **Note:** many commentators have said the injustices occurring in the Irish cases could not now be repeated, because of PACE. This is erroneous. Today, suspected terrorists are still held under the PTA.

m. The danger of allowing the jury to convict on uncorroborated confession evidence.

n. Over-anxiety on the part of the police to secure a conviction, including a preparedness to fabricate evidence, in cases where there is a public outcry against the perpetrators. All these cases involve Irish or black defendants.

o. Over-willingness in certain Court of Appeal judges to believe prosecution evidence, probably caused by the fact that the majority of them are recruited from prosecuting counsel.

p. Limited powers of the Court of Appeal: an inability to provide a full rehearing.

They drew attention to the difficult constitutional issues involved in establishing the relationship between the Authority and the Court of Appeal, such as the need to prevent the Authority from usurping the courts' functions.

Civil Appeals

Appeals from Magistrates' Courts.

1. Appeals to the Crown Court. As in criminal cases, appeal lies to the Crown Court, *e.g.* in licensing cases.

2. Appeals to the High Court by way of case stated, to the Queen's Bench Division and the Family Division (Divisional Courts).

3. Appeals to the High Court in family cases. In certain family matters, appeal lies on fact or law to the Divisional Court of the Family Division. The Court may substitute any order made by the magistrates or remit for rehearing.

Appeals from the County Court and High Court from 2000

As with most of its newest reforms of the English legal system, the Government explained the rationale behind its new regime, in force in May 2000, in its 1998 white paper, *Modernising Justice*. The resulting procedure is contained in the Access to Justice Act 1999, in the Civil Procedure Rules 1998, the amended Rules of the Supreme Court and in various practice directions. The whole regime is explained by the Court of Appeal (Civil Division) in *Tanfern Ltd v. Cameron-Macdonald and another* (2000).

The Government explained, in *Modernising Justice*, that they planned to achieve their objectives of proportionality and efficiency (the same as in the rest of civil procedure) by

- "diverting from the Court of Appeal those cases which, by their nature, do not require the attention of the most senior judges in the country.
- Making various changes to the working methods of the Court, which will enable it to deploy its resources more efficiently and effectively."

to enable the Court to deal with the increased workload which would result from the Human Rights Act 1998 (brought into force in 2000). Their guiding principles are now:

- Permission to appeal will only be given where the court considers that an appeal would have a real prospect of success.
- In normal circumstances, more than one appeal cannot be justified.
- There should be no automatic right to appeal. Leave (now called permission) would be required in virtually all appeals to the Court of Appeal.

Jurisdiction

The Government, after consultation, decided routes of appeal should be as follows:

- In fact track cases heard by a district judge, appeal lies to a circuit judge.
- In fast track cases heard by a circuit judge, appeal lies to a High Court judge.
- In multi-track cases, appeals against *final orders* lie to the Court of Appeal, regardless of the original judge.
- In multi-track cases, appeals against a *procedural decision* of a district judge will be to a circuit judge; decisions by a Master or circuit judge lie to a High Court judge and from procedural decisions of a High Court judge lie to the Court of Appeal.
- Exceptional cases involving important points of principle or which affect a number of litigants may go straight to the Court of Appeal.

Composition

Changes to the composition, procedures, working methods and management of the Court of Appeal (Civil Division) are designed to help it operate more efficiently:

- Under the Access of Justice Act 1999, the Court of Appeal can now consist of any number of judges, according to the importance and complexity of the case.
- There will be more emphasis on case management and a more coherent I.T. infrastructure.

Approach

Generally, every appeal is limited to a review of the decision of the lower court, unless Practice Direction provides otherwise or the court considered that in the circumstances of an individual appeal, it would be in the interests of justice to hold a rehearing.

Grounds The appeal court will only allow an appeal where the lower court was wrong (in substance) or where it was unjust because of a *serious* procedural or other irregularity. Under the new procedure, the decision of the lower court attracts a much greater significance.

Recording decisions The new emphasis on the importance of the first instance decision makes it all the more important for decision to be recorded accurately.

Powers

The general rule is that all appeal courts have all the powers of the lower court. It also has the power to affirm, set aside or vary any order or judgment of the lower court, to refer any claim or issue for determination by the lower court, to order a new trial or hearing and to make a costs order.

In October 2000, small claims appeals were placed on the same footing as other civil appeals. The appellant must obtain permission. The appeal is an oral review, not a rehearing.

Second Appeals

The Court of Appeal in *Tanfern* said Parliament had made it clear in the Access to Justice Act 1999 that second appeals would now be a rarity. The decision of the first appeal court should be given primacy, unless the Court of Appeal itself considered that the appeal would raise an important point of principle or practice or, that there was some other compelling reason for it to hear a second appeal.

The Court of Appeal (Civil Division) sat in Wales (Cardiff) for the first time in 1999.

Appeals from the Court of Appeal to the House of Lords.

An appeal lies from any judgment of the Court of Appeal. An application for leave must be made first to the Court of Appeal and, if refused, may be made to the House of Lords.

Appeals are normally heard by five Law Lords. The parties must each lodge a printed "case," supposedly being a succinct statement of the arguments below and of the issues before the House. Theoretically, all Law Lords will have read this "case" and the judgments in the court below in advance of the hearing. This emphasis on written argument has been used to reduce oral argument before the House. Judgment is normally reserved and their Lordships' opinions delivered some days or weeks later. Any orders made are, technically, High Court orders, as the House has no machinery for enforcement.

References to the European Court of Justice

Article 234 EEC concerns references to the European Court of Justice by domestic courts of Member States:

"(1) The Court of Justice shall have jurisdiction to give preliminary rulings concerning:

(a) the interpretation of the Treaty;
(b) the validity and interpretation of acts of the institutions of the Community and of the ECB;
(c) the interpretation of the statutes of bodies established by an Act of the Council, where those statutes so provide.

(2) Where such a question is raised before any court or tribunal of a Member State, that court or tribunal may, if it considers that a decision on the question is necessary to enable it to give judgment, request the Court of Justice to give a ruling thereon.

(3) Where any such question is raised in a case pending before a court or tribunal of a Member State, against whose decisions there is no judicial remedy under national law, that court or tribunal shall bring the matter before the Court of Justice."

Points to note about Article 234 are these:

(a) Any judicial or quasi-judicial body may refer, however lowly. For instance, magistrates' courts and tribunals.
(b) The "question" may be raised by the parties or the court but only the court may make the reference.
(c) The ruling is *preliminary* only in the sense that the case then goes back to the original court for it to apply the law to the facts. Obviously, the ECJ's rulings on E.C. law, etc., are final.
(d) The ECJ will not answer hypothetical questions.
(e) Facts should normally be found before reference but there may be exceptional cases.
(f) The ECJ has accepted the doctrine of *acte clair*. This means that a point need not be referred if it is "reasonably clear and free from doubt."
(g) References under Article 234 are discretionary, except where there is no judicial remedy against the domestic court's decision. In that instance, an *obligation* to refer arises under Article 234(3).

6. EXAM TIPS, MODEL QUESTIONS AND ANSWER GUIDES

EXAM TIPS

Revision: How?

Start early in the year. You have a three month summer holiday, so use Easter to revise hard, otherwise you may waste the summer (or all next year!) revising for a resit. Draw up a revision timetable and stick to it. You will underestimate the time taken to revise. If your lecture notes and others are scrappy, you *may* find it helpful to make revision notes.

Revision: What?

You should aim to know the whole course fairly well and, as much of it as possible, in greater depth. *Question spotting* is very difficult in E.L.S., as there can be so many different permutations of topics, *e.g.* "the adversarial process" includes civil and criminal trial and pre-trial; legal profession might be combined with judiciary or with legal services, etc. It helps, however, to *know your own course*. Know the topics your course teachers have emphasised in *your year*. Topicality means past papers are, in some respects, unhelpful. Whereas in 1989, I set questions on the Civil Justice Review, the obvious topics of 2000 are the Labour Government's reforms of legal services and civil justice (implementation of Woolf). Do *not* revise from notes for other courses and do not fool yourself that this *Nutshell* is anything but a revision aid, a comforter. It is not a substitute for having worked hard and, in this subject, *read widely*, throughout the year. Beware that it may omit things emphasised in *your* course, *e.g.* bail, family courts, Ministry of Justice.

Know the *approach* of your course, as well as its content, *e.g.* at Kingston, E.L.S. for law undergraduates is highly critical, sometimes political and always analytical and discursive, much more so than this *Nutshell*, but the ability to appreciate E.L.S. in the context of this approach comes from wide reading. E.L.S. for undergraduates in non-law courses and students on other courses, is usually much more factual, and a "tools for the trade" approach.

In the Exam

Organise your time. Every year I groan over a handful of 2A students who achieve 3rds or fails because they have answered two and a half or three questions instead of four. Think about it. If you answer three instead of four, you must achieve an *average* of 66 per cent in those three, just to attain an examination mark of 50 per cent (*just* a 2B). Divide the exam time by the number of answers required and force yourself to move on when time is up. Leave ample space between answers to add points, even in neat note form, to your earlier answers, if you can spare 10 minutes at the end. Lecturers always say and some students never seem to understand the simple point that it is much easier to gain 30 marks on answering a new question than to add 30 to a near-complete one. *Do not waffle. Write clearly.* Try rollerball or superior ballpoint. See which is quicker and neater. Fountain pens are too slow. Bad writing is *bound* to affect the markers, as they cannot get the "gist," the "flow" of an argument, even if they can slowly interpret it, word by word. If your handwriting is bad, get help urgently, in college or privately. *If English is not your first language* practise it by getting as much of your written English checked as you can persuade people to mark (on any topic). Again, if you need remedial help, your college may provide it. In the exam, you need time for mental translation. Time will be your enemy so make every word count. Waffle is even more dangerous for you than a native student.

Answer the question set. If you panic and mis-read a question on juries as one on magistrates, you may get 0. If you "write all you know" where a critical analysis or a particular approach is needed, you *may*, but only if you are lucky, scrape a pass, however detailed you are and however much you have learned. Plan and present your answer and *only* include that which is required. Do not be tempted to demonstrate knowledge just because you have revised it.

Be authoritative. The trouble with this subject is that every *Sun* reader has an opinion on the jury or the legal profession. You must substantiate your beliefs with fact and authoritative opinion. Most opinions have found written expression in some text, article or committee report, sometimes in many, but do not invent sources/quotations. Your examiner will know better. Being authoritative comes from *wide reading*, not a *Nutshell*. Be *original*: very difficult but the more so the better. Reach your own *informed* opinions. Draw on your own observation of courts and tribunals. They provide hours of free entertainment on a wet Wednesday afternoon. Read a quality newspaper daily. Search for new commentaries and articles in law journals.

QUESTIONS AND ANSWERS

I thoroughly disapprove of model answers to questions on the English legal system for law undergraduates. The questions I set may be *very* different from those set in your course, so beware. I usually set questions which require the student to know the facts but, more importantly, to use imagination and express an informed, substantiated opinion. The concept of a "model" answer is nonsense and the danger of such "models" is that they may stifle imagination. I mark questions without a preconceived idea of "the" answer, although there may be only one legitimate set of parameters.

These are only my suggestions below. You can find different ways of arguing the same or evidence to argue the opposite. Do not be daunted. My opinion is worth no more than yours, provided yours is relevant and *substantiated*.

QUESTION 1

Comment critically on the use of lay people as decision makers in the English legal system.

Answer Notes

This question is so wide it provides ample scope but could give you enough rope to hang yourself, if you fail to identify what is required. "Lay people" includes magistrates *and* juries *plus* tribunal members and arbitrators. "Decision makers" excludes expert witnesses. Comment critically does not mean criticise any more or less than a theatre critic. If you think their use should be protected then say so and why. "The use" suggests non-use. If not used, what is the alternative? Professionals?

Use of lay justices. Cheap. Unique. The system would collapse without them. Pros and cons of lay justices or district judges. Obvious advantages of having "ordinary people" judge or sentence most petty offenders and hear family and juvenile cases but are they "ordinary people?" Problems of achieving a balanced bench, socially, politically, occupationally, let alone in intelligence. Use of lay people O.K. if they are trained to understand their job without over-training and if not dominated by the professionals in court, especially clerks.

Use of jurors. Traditional civil libertarian support. Democracy, etc. Devlin, Blackstone BUT cons.: decline in jury use in civil cases due to lack of confidence (reasons) and very few criminal cases use jury trial so how can it be a significant guardian of civil liberties, etc.? Roskill report suggested abolition in fraud cases. Not followed but thin end of the wedge? Like magistrates, advantage is supposed to be trial by representatives of the man in the street. Randomness and representativeness eroded by statute, excuses, vetting.

Use of tribunal panel and arbitrators. Advantage: expertise and, in some tribunals, *e.g.* industrial, a balanced panel must instil some confidence. O.K. so long as sufficient law injected by lawyer chairman.

Alternatives. Professional judges. Pros and cons. Decide for yourself.

QUESTION 2

Is the system of selection and training of the judiciary likely to produce judges fitted to perform their constitutional role as independent, impartial arbiters?

Answer Notes

Expand on what you understand by "constitutional role" and "independence," etc. Political? Aloof from corruption and outside influences? Define impartial. Analyse system of appointment, selection and training in the light of all this. Make only relevant points and link them to the question, continually.

Selection. Predominantly from Bar, especially superior judiciary. No career judiciary in England, as in Europe, so circuit judges cannot necessarily expect promotion to High Court. Bar elitist, expensive to enter. Difficult to find a tenancy. Anachronistic rules mark it out from solicitors/public. Cloistered socialisation. High Court judges selected from small number of eligible Q.C.s. Hardly surprising most superior judges come from higher social classes, public school and Oxbridge. Now, throughout 1990s, Lord Chancellor has been criticised for recruitment policies that are racist, sexist and exclude solicitors. How can this narrow social background fit them for impartially judging all social classes and understanding the evidence before them? The C.L.S.A. obviously gives scope for more solicitor appointments. Will this have any impact? What do *you* think? Do you have any alternatives? Would *Justice*'s suggestion of appointing academics help? Would a career judiciary help?

Selection by Lord Chancellor, political appointee. Dubious, constitutionally, as a breach of separation of powers. Open to accusations of political bias, even if recent Lord Chancellors have acted independently. The E.L.S. is elsewhere concerned with appearances: "justice should be seen to be done." Few judges now are ex-M.P.s, as at the turn of the century, however.

Even if judges are party politically independent, they are still likely to hold conservative, established views because they are selected by Lord Chancellor and senior civil servants; average age on appointment is high. History of judicial activity in administrative law, labour law, civil liberties, as recounted by Griffith. Thus, even if party politically impartial, they come from a limited social/political group. Will the new Labour Government eventually create a Judicial Appointments Commission? If so, how would you like it to be consituted? What criteria should it use for selecting judges?

Alternatives? *Justice* (1992) suggested a Judicial Appointments Commission. Career judiciary? Use your imagination.

Training. Precious little. Experience on the job. Otherwise experience as an advocate, the antithesis of training. *Justice* report and judicial studies working party said they should be trained. On what? Use your imagination, *e.g.* sociology, courtroom psychology, criminology, penology, even law, for those from the specialist Bar. Civil Justice Review recommended a more interventionist judicial role so should be training in case management techniques. Also, if they are to be more interventionist in helping unrepresented parties in the lower courts, they need training for this too. Could they, conceivably, be trained to be impartial?

EXAMINATION CHECKLIST

1. The English Legal System is the most fast changing area of law by far. Have you made sure that the information you've been revising from is totally up to date? This book was proof read in Autumn 2000. Have things changed since then? Surf through the Lord Chancellor's Department website (www.open.gov.uk/lcd) and see if there is anything you have missed. Especially click on "What's new?", "Press releases" and "Consultation papers". Go into the Home Office website (www.homeoffice.gov.uk) and scroll through the press releases, starting with the most recent. Click on any titles which appear relevant. If time, surf the Legal Services Commission website similarly (www.legalservices.gov.uk).
2. Have you familiarised yourself with critiques of various elements of the system? Some are contained in this book but look out for those which have appeared since January 2001. Especially good courses of brief, pithy articles and editorials are the New Law Journal and Legal Action. These two are also perfect sources for keeping up to date so browse through editions since January 2001.
3. Do not forget *The Times* law reports are another great source of brand new case law.
4. Have you understood which courts are civil and which criminal and what the difference in terminology is between the two? Never confuse these in an exam answer, it makes you look monumentally daft.
5. Are you familiar with the underlying philosophy of the "Woolf reforms" (Civil Procedure Rules 1998)? Do you know the outline framework of civil procedure now and why the reforms were made? Remember to look at the section on civil appeals too.

6. Have you understood that legal aid has been replaced? Why? What body replaced the Legal Aid Board? By what framework are civil legal services administered? What is the job of the new Regional Legal Services Committees? Remember legal services are now provided by contracted (franchised) solicitors and non-solicitor agencies. Remember this ensures that the providers are experts but the criticism is that the outlets of legal services will be too limited to provide proper access to justice. People will be turned away from solicitors who have too big a caseload or whose contract does not cover the client's problem. The Lord Chancellor intended most civil legal aid to be replaced by conditional fees. What are the pros and cons?

7. Who now administers funded advice and representation in criminal cases? Who are the providers? Have we established a system of salaried defenders? When? Why? What are the criticisms of such a system?

8. At the time of writing, the Law Society was redrafting its practice rules to make it easier to become as solicitor advocate. This follows the opening up of rights of audience by the Access to Justice Act 1999. What does a solicitor now have to do to qualify to appear in the higher courts? How many solicitor advocates are there now? The Law Society can provide you with that information. Do you think they will pose a threat to the 9,000 barristers in independent practice?

9. Remember that professional magistrates, formerly known as stipendiaries, are part of a unified bench throughout England and Wales, since the Access to Justice Act 1999 and they have been renamed district judges (magistrates' courts). The other magistrates are called lay justices or J.P.s. They are not professionals but must sit for at least 26 half days per year.

10. At the time of writing, Lord Justice Auld was conducting his review of the criminal courts. He will report in February 2001. Look at his website for news (www.criminal-courts-review.org.uk.). Learn his list of key recommendations and find out whether they have been implemented, via this website or the sources listed above.

11. Remember the traditional critiques of the judiciary: too Oxbridge, middle/upper class, too male and mostly too old. Do not say they are Conservative. That point is out

of date. Has the Lord Chancellor done anything to reform the system of recruiting and selecting judges recently? Remember that the system of "secret soundings", consulting existing members of the judiciary on a candidate, angers many critics such as the Law Society. Many people want to see the establishment of a Legal Services Commission, to advise the Lord Chancellor or replace his role in recruitment. The present Lord Chancellor said he would think about this. Has he done anything? Look at his website.

The Court Structure

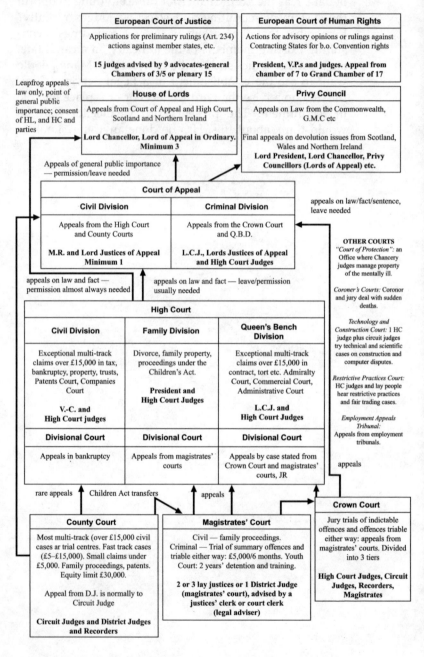

European Court of Justice	European Court of Human Rights
Applications for preliminary rulings (Art. 234) actions against member states, etc. **15 judges advised by 9 advocates-general Chambers of 3/5 or plenary 15**	Actions for advisory opinions or rulings against Contracting States for b.o. Convention rights **President, V.P.s and judges. Appeal from chamber of 7 to Grand Chamber of 17**

Leapfrog appeals — law only, point of general public importance; consent of HL, and HC and parties

House of Lords	Privy Council
Appeals from Court of Appeal and High Court, Scotland and Northern Ireland **Lord Chancellor, Lord of Appeal in Ordinary. Minimum 3**	Appeals on Law from the Commonwealth, G.M.C etc Final appeals on devolution issues from Scotland, Wales and Northern Ireland **Lord President, Lord Chancellor, Privy Councillors (Lords of Appeal) etc.**

Appeals of general public importance — permission/leave needed

Court of Appeal

appeals on law/fact/sentence, leave needed

Civil Division	Criminal Division
Appeals from the High Court and County Courts **M.R. and Lord Justices of Appeal Minimum 1**	Appeals from the Crown Court and Q.B.D. **L.C.J., Lords Justices of Appeal and High Court Judges**

appeals on law and fact — permission almost always needed

appeals on law and fact — leave/permission usually needed

High Court

Civil Division	Family Division	Queen's Bench Division
Exceptional multi-track claims over £15,000 in tax, bankruptcy, property, trusts, Patents Court, Companies Court **V.-C. and High Court judges**	Divorce, family property, proceedings under the Children's Act. **President and High Court Judges**	Exceptional multi-track claims over £15,000 in contract, tort etc. Admiralty Court, Commercial Court, Administrative Court **L.C.J. and High Court Judges**
Divisional Court	**Divisional Court**	**Divisional Court**
Appeals in bankruptcy	Appeals from magistrates' courts	Appeals by case stated from Crown Court and magistrates' courts, JR

OTHER COURTS

"Court of Protection": an Office where Chancery judges manage property of the mentally ill.

Coroner's Courts: Coronor and jury deal with sudden deaths.

Technology and Construction Court: 1 HC judge plus circuit judges try technical and scientific cases on construction and computer disputes.

Restrictive Practices Court: HC judges and lay people hear restrictive practices and fair trading cases.

Employment Appeals Tribunal: Appeals from employment tribunals.

appeals

rare appeals   Children Act transfers   appeals

County Court	Magistrates' Court
Most multi-track (over £15,000 civil cases ar trial centres. Fast track cases (£5–£15,000). Small claims under £5,000. Family proceedings, patents. Equity limit £30,000. Appeal from D.J. is normally to Circuit Judge **Circuit Judges and District Judges and Recorders**	Civil — family proceedings. Criminal — Trial of summary offences and triable either way: £5,000/6 months. Youth Court: 2 years' detention and training. **2 or 3 lay justices or 1 District Judge (magistrates' court), advised by a justices' clerk or court clerk (legal adviser)**

Crown Court

Jury trials of indictable offences and offences triable either way: appeals from magistrates' courts. Divided into 3 tiers

High Court Judges, Circuit Judges, Recorders, Magistrates

INDEX

Notes

Notes